Collins
gem

C000043766

Croatian
phrasebook

Consultant
Milorad Krystanovich

First published 2007
Copyright © HarperCollins Publishers
Reprint 10 9 8 7 6 5 4 3 2 1 0
Typeset by Davidson Pre-Press, Glasgow
Printed in Malaysia by Imago

www.collins.co.uk

ISBN 13 978-0-00-724678-6
ISBN 10 0-00-724678-1

Using your phrasebook

Your *Collins Gem Phrasebook* is designed to help you locate the exact phrase you need, when you need it, whether on holiday or for business. If you want to adapt the phrases, you can easily see where to substitute your own words using the dictionary section, and the clear, full-colour layout gives you direct access to the different topics.

The Gem Phrasebook includes:
- Over 70 topics arranged thematically. Each phrase is accompanied by a simple pronunciation guide which eliminates any problems pronouncing foreign words.

- A top ten tips section to safeguard against any cultural faux pas, giving essential dos and don'ts for situations involving local customs or etiquette.

- Practical hints to make your stay trouble free, showing you where to go and what to do when dealing with everyday matters such as travel or hotels and offering valuable tourist information.

- Face to face sections so that you understand what is being said to you. These example mini-dialogues give you a good idea of what to expect from a real conversation.

- Common announcements and messages you may hear, ensuring that you never miss the important information you need to know when out and about.

- A clearly laid-out 3000-word dictionary means you will never be stuck for words.

- A basic grammar section which will enable you to build on your phrases.

- A list of public holidays to avoid being caught out by unexpected opening and closing hours, and to make sure you don't miss the celebrations!

It's worth spending time before you embark on your travels just looking through the topics to see what is covered and becoming familiar with what might be said to you.

Whatever the situation, your *Gem Phrasebook* is sure to help!

Contents

Pronouncing Croatian

Spelling and pronouncing Croatian are easy once you know the few basic rules. Each letter is pronounced separately and each word is spelt as it is pronounced. In shorter words, you usually stress the first syllable. In longer words, you rarely stress the last syllable. Each part of a word is pronounced without reducing or contracting sounds.

The Croatian alphabet has 30 letters. Vowel sounds are pure and tend to be longer than in English.

Croatian	sounds like	example	pronunciation
a	**fa**ther	**ka**va	kah-vah
e	**te**n	**be**z	bez
i	**see**k	**pi**vo	pee-vo
o	**au**burn	**vo**ća	vau-cha
u	**foo**d	**mu**zej	moo-zey
ao	c**ow**	**če**kaonica	tche-kow-nee-tsah
io	n**eo**n	**di**o	deeo

The pronunciation of the consonants below is similar to their English equivalents:

b bed, **d** dog, **f** fish, **g** good, **k** duck, **l** lock, **m** man, **n** not, **p** top, **s** some, **t** talk, **v** vase, **z** zero.

Consonants to watch out for are:

Croatian	sounds like	example	pronunciation
h	**h**ave	**k**uhati	koo-hah-tee
j	**y**es	**j**utro	yoo-trau
r	**r**ose (but rolled)	**s**ir	seer
lj	mi**lli**on	**lj**ubav	lyoo-bahv
nj	ca**ny**on	pu**nj**enje	poo-nye-nye
c	pi**zz**a (never as **k** or **s**)	**dj**eca	dye-tsa
č	**ch**air	**č**ek	check
ć	na**tu**re	du**ć**ani	doo-chah-nee
đ	**d**uke	**đ**ak	dahk
dž	**j**umper	**dž**ep	jep
š	**sh**oe	tro**š**ak	trau-shahk
ž	plea**s**ure	**ž**ivjeli	zhee-vye-lee

Take care with the following combinations when j sounds like the English y:

Croatian	sounds like	example	pronunciation
aj	m**y**	kr**aj**	kray
ja	**ya**rd	pri**ja**viti	pree-ya-vee-tee
ji	**ye**	dragul**ji**	drah-goo-lyee
oj	b**oy**	br**oj**	brauy
ju	**yo**u	kompj**u**tor	kaum-pyoo-taur
dj	**d**ue	**dj**ečica	dye-chee-tsah

Top ten tips

••

1   In Croatia the blood alcohol limit for driving
    is 0%.

2   It is not necessary to tip taxi drivers. In expensive
    restaurants a tip of 10-15% is expected, while
    café and bar bills can be rounded up.

3   Croatia has a long tradition of naturist tourism;
    the first naturist holidays date from 1934.

4   The Italian influence is apparent in many
    historical sites (churches, cathedrals, squares,
    city walls, citadels, old houses etc) all over Istria,
    Kvarner and Dalmatia. Italian is the official
    second language in Istria and the influence of
    the language is apparent in the Adriatic coastal
    areas as well.

5   In Croatia, holidays are celebrated with typical
    national dishes: cod is prepared for Christmas
    Eve and Good Friday and pork or turkey is eaten
    on New Year's Day.

6   If you are offered something to eat, it is more polite to say 'I cannot' (**ne mogu**) than 'no thank you' (**ne, hvala vam**).

7   If you are invited to join your neighbour/a local on their veranda or in their garden for a drink, it is polite to accept and spend a little time chatting with them.

8   In the old town of Dubrovnik you will find lots of restaurant and shop signs advertised on the street lamps.

9   People normally shake hands upon meeting and parting and they also kiss each other if they are relatives or in a close relationship.

10 There are some signs of Mediterranean characteristics in Croatians: people speak loudly in the green markets and promenades and sometimes can be noisy in the streets and on the beaches as well.

Talking to p

Hello/goodbye, yes/no

Croats can be quite formal in their greeting. If you don't know someone well, the best greeting is **dobar dan** (literally good day). If you are slightly unsure how formal to be **bok** is a good option.

Please	**Molim**
	mau-lee-m
Thanks	**Hvala (velika)**
(very much)	**hva**-la (**ve**-lee-kah)
You're welcome!	**Nema na čemu**
	ne-ma nah **che**-moo
Yes	**Da**
	dah
No	**Ne**
	ne
Yes, please	**Da, molim vas**
	dah, **mau**-lee-m vas
No, thanks	**Ne, hvala**
	ne, **hva**-la

11

	U redu!
	oo **re**-doo!
Sir/Mr...	**Gospodine...**
	gaus-p**au**-dee-ne...
Madam/Mrs.../ Ms...	**Gospođo...**
	gaus-pau-jau...
Miss	**Gospođice...**
	gaus-pau-jee-tse...
Good morning	**Dobro jutro**
	dau-broh **yoo**-troh
Goodbye	**Doviđenja**
	dau-vee-je-nya
Hi/Bye	**Bok**
	bau-ck
See you later	**Vidimo se kasnije**
	vee-dee-mau se **kas**-nee-ye
Good evening	**Dobra večer**
	daub-ra **vech**-er
Goodnight	**Laku noć**
	lah-cku nau-ch
Good afternoon	**Dobar dan**
	dau-bar dahn
Excuse me!/Sorry!	**Oprostite!/Žao mi je!**
	aup-**rau**-stee-te!/**zh-ow** mee ye!
Excuse me! (to get past in a crowd)	**Ispričavam se!**
	ees-**pri**-cha-vam se!
How are you?	**Kako ste?**
	kah-ckau ste?

Fine, thanks	**Dobro, hvala**
	dau-broh, **hva**-la
And you?	**A vi?**
	a vee?
I don't understand	**Ne razumijem**
	ne rah-**zoo**-mee-yem
I don't speak	**Ne govorim hrvatski**
Croatian	ne **gau**-vau-reem hr-**vaht**-skee

Key phrases

Where do you live?	**Gdje živite?**
(formal)	gd-ye **zhee**-vee-te?
(informal)	**Gdje živiš?**
	gd-ye **zhee**-veesh?
Where is...?	**Gdje je...?**
	gd-ye ye...?
Where are...?	**Gdje su...?**
	gd-ye soo...?
the museum	**muzej**
	moo-zey
the station	**kolodvor/postaja**
	kau-lav-dvaur/**pau**-sta-yah
the shops	**dućani**
	doo-**chah**-nee
the houses	**kuće**
	koo-che

13

Do you like...?	**Da li volite?**
(formal)	da lee **vau**-lee-te?
(informal)	**Da li voliš...?**
	da lee **vau**-leesh...?
What do you want?	**Što želite?**
(formal)	sh-tau **zhe**-lee-te?
(informal)	**Što želiš?**
	sh-tau **zhe**-leesh?
The wine is good	**Vino je dobro**
	vee-nau ye **daub**-rau
The coffee is very good	**Kava je jako dobra**
	kah-vah ye **yah**-ko **dau**-brah
The beer is excellent	**Pivo je izvrsno**
	pee-vau ye **eez**-vrs-nau
Do you have...?	**Imate li...?**
	ee-ma-te lee...?
Do you have a timetable?	**Imate li vozni red?**
	ee-ma-te lee **vauz**-nee red?
Do you have a room?	**Imate li sobu?**
	ee-ma-te lee **sau**-boo?
Do you have milk?	**Imate li mlijeka?**
	ee-ma-te lee **mlee**-ye-kah?
I'd like...	**Ja bih...**
	ya beeh...
We'd like...	**Mi bismo...**
	mee **bee**-smau...
a ticket/a stamp	**kartu/marku**
	kar-too/**mar**-ckoo

a room/a bottle	**sobu**/**bocu**
	sau-boo/**bau**-tsoo
some wine	**nešto vina**
	nesh-toh vee-na
some fruit	**nešto voća**
	nesh-toh vau-cha
some biscuits	**nešto keksa**
	nesh-toh **kek**-sa
some crisps	**nešto čipsa**
	nesh-toh **chip**-sa
I'd like an ice cream	**Ja bih sladoled**
	ya beeh **sla**-dau-led
We'd like to go home	**Mi bismo išli doma**
	mee **bee**-smau **eesh**-lee dau-ma
Another/ Some more... (singular)/(plural)	**Još jedno**/**Još molim**...
	yaush **yed**-nau/ yaush **mau**-leem...
Some more bread	**Još kruha molim**
	yaush **kroo**-ha **mau**-leem
Some more glasses	**Još čaša molim**
	yaush **tcha**-sha **mau**-leem
Another espresso	**Još jedan espreso**
	yaush **yed**-an e-**spre**-soh
Another beer	**Još jedno pivo**
	yaush **yed**-nau **pee**-vau
Some more water	**Još vode molim**
	yaush **vau**-de **mau**-leem

How much is it?	**Koliko je to?**	
	kau-lee-ckau ye tau?	
How much does it cost?	**Koliko to košta?**	
	kau-lee-koh tau **kaush**-ta?	
large (neut.)	**veliko**	
	ve-lee-koh	
(masc.)	**veliki**	
	ve-lee-kee	
(fem.)	**velika**	
	ve-lee-kah	
small (neut.)	**malo**	
	ma-lau	
(masc.)	**mali**	
	ma-lee	
(fem.)	**mala**	
	ma-lah	
with	**s/sa**	
	s/sa	
without	**bez**	
	bez	
Where is...?	**Gdje je...?**	
	gdye ye...?	
Where are...?	**Gdje su...?**	
	gdje soo...?	
the nearest	**najbliže**	
	nay-blee-zhe	
How do I get...?	**Kako mogu doći...?**	
	ka-koh **mau**-goo **dau**-chee...?	

to the museum	**do muzeja**
	dau **moo**-ze-yah
to the station	**do kolodvora**
	dau **kau**-lau-dvau-rah
to Rijeka	**do Rijeke**
	dau ree-**ye**-cke
There is.../	**Ima...**
There are...	**ee**-mah...
There isn't.../	**Nema...**
There aren't any...	**ne**-mah...
When?	**Kad?**
	kad?
At what time...?	**U koliko sati...?**
	oo **kau**-lee-ckau **sa**tee...?
today	**danas**
	dah-nas
tomorrow	**sutra**
	soo-tra
Can I...?	**mogu li...?**
	mau-goo lee...?
smoke	**pušiti**
	poo-shee-tee
taste it	**probati**
	prau-ba-tee
How does this work?	**Kako to radi?**
	ka-ckau tau **ra**-dee?
What does this mean?	**Što to znači?**
	shtau tau **zna**-tchee?

Signs and notices

ulaz	entrance
izlaz	exit
otvoreno	open
zatvoreno	closed
vruće	hot
hladno	cold
povucite	pull
gurnite	push
nepitka voda	not drinking water
pažnja molimo	caution please
zabranjeno	forbidden
slobodno	free, vacant
zauzeto	engaged
pazi oštar pas	beware of the dog
gospoda (Muški WC)	gents
gospođe (Ženski WC)	ladies
ne radi, van uporabe	out of order
blagajna	cash desk
iznajmljuje se/ u najam	for hire/for rent
kupanje nije dozvoljeno	no bathing
prodaje se	for sale
rasprodaja	sale
podrum	basement

prizemlje	ground floor
dizalo	lift
krug	ring
tisak	press
slobodne sobe	rooms available
nema soba	no vacancies
izlaz u slučaju opasnosti	emergency exit
privatno	private
vlakovi	to the trains
prodaja karata	tickets
vozni red	timetable
stoj	stop
ovjerite vašu kartu	validate your ticket
izgubljena prtljaga	left luggage
dolazak	arrivals
odlazak	departures
peron	platform
za nepušače	non-smoking
za pušače	smoking
pušenje zabranjeno	no smoking

Polite expressions

• •

There are two forms of address in Croatian: formal
(vi) and informal (ti). You should always stick to the
formal until you are invited to use the informal.

The lunch was delicious	**Ručak je bio sjajan**
	roo-tch-ack ye beeo **sya**-yan
The dinner was delicious	**Večera je bila sjajna**
	ve-tche-ra ye **bee**-la **sya**-ynah
This is a gift for you	**Ovo je poklon za vas**
	au-vau ye **pau**-cklaun za vas
Pleased to meet you	**Drago mi je (što smo se upoznali)**
	drah-gau mee ye (shto smo se oo-**pauz**-na-lee)
This is my husband	**Ovo je moj muž**
	au-vau ye mauy mooj
This is my wife	**Ovo je moja žena**
	au-vau ye **mau**-ya **zhe**-na
Enjoy your holiday!	**Uživajte u odmoru!**
	oo-zhee-vay-te oo **aud**-mau-roo!
or	**Uživaj u odmoru!**
	oo-zhee-vay oo **aud**-mau-roo!

Celebrations

• •

I'd like to wish you... (masc.)	**Poželio bih vam...**
	pau-**zhe**-leeo beeh vam...
(fem.)	**Poželjela bih vam...**
	pau-**zhe**-lye-la beeh vam...
Happy Birthday!	**Sretan rođendan!**
	sre-tahn **rau**-jen-dahn!

Happy Anniversary!	**Sretnu obljetnicu!**
	sret-noo **aub**-lye-tnee-tsoo!
Merry Christmas!	**Sretan Božić!**
	sre-tahn **bau**-zhee-ch!
Happy New Year!	**Sretnu Novu Godinu!**
	sret-nuh **nau**-vu **gau**-dee-nuh!
Happy Easter!	**Sretan Uskrs!**
	sre-tahn **oo**-skrs!
Have a good trip!	**Sretan put!**
	sre-tahn poot!

Making friends

••

In this section we have used the familiar form "**ti**" for the questions.

FACE TO FACE

A **Kako ti je ime?**
kah-koh tee ye **ee**-me?
What is your name?

B **Moje ime je…**
mau-ye **ee**-me ye…
My name is…

A **Odakle si?**
au-dah-kle see?
Where are you from?

B **Ja sam Englez** (masc.)/**Engleskinja** (fem.), **iz Londona**
ya sahm **en**-gle-z/**en**-gles-kee-nya, eez **laun**-dau-nah
I am English, from London

A **Drago mi je!**
drah-gau mee ye!
Pleased to meet you!

How old are you?	**Koliko imaš godina?**	
	kau-lee-ckoh **ee**-mash **gau**-dee-nah?	
I'm ... years old	**Ja imam ... godina**	
	ya **ee**-mahm ... **gau**-dee-nah	
Where do you live?	**Gdje živiš?**	
	gdye **jee**-veesh?	
Where do you live?	**Gdje živite?**	
(plural)	gdye **zhee**-vee-te?	
I live in London	**Ja živim u Londonu**	
	ya **zhee**-veem oo **laun**-daun-oo	
We live in Glasgow	**Mi živimo u Glasgowu**	
	mee **zhee**-vee-mau oo **glaz**-gau-voo	
I'm at school	**Ja sam još u školi**	
	ya sam yaush oo **shkoh**-lee	
I work	**Ja radim**	
	ya **rah**-deem	
I'm retired	**Ja sam u mirovini**	
	ya sahm oo mee-**rau**-vee-nee	
I'm ... married	**Ja sam ... udana/oženjen**	
(fem.)/(masc.)	ya sahm ... **oo**-dah-nah/**au**-zhe-nyen	
divorced	**razvedena/razveden**	
(fem.)/(masc.)	**rahz**-ve-de-nah/**rahz**-ve-den	

22

widowed (fem.)/(masc.)	**udovica/udovac** **oo**-dau-vee-tsa/**oo**-dau-vahts
I have...	**Ja imam...** ya **ee**-mahm...
a boyfriend	**momka** **maum**-cka
a girlfriend	**curu** **tsoo**-roo
a partner	**partnera** **par**-tne-ra
I have ... children	**Ja imam ... djece** ya **ee**-mam ... dye-tseh
I have no children	**Ja nemam djece** ya **ne**-mam **dye**-tseh
I'm here...	**Ja sam tu...** ya sahm too...
on holiday	**na odmoru** nah **aud**-mau-roo
on business	**poslovno** **paus**-lauv-nau
for the weekend	**za vikend** za **veeck**-end
What do you do?	**Što vi radite?** sht-au vee **ra**-dee-te?
Do you like your job?	**Volite li svoj posao?** **vau**-lee-te lee svoy **pau**-sow?
I'm...	**Ja sam...** ya sam...

a doctor (masc.)	**liječnik**
	lee-**yetch**-neeck
(fem.)	**liječnica**
	lee-**yetch**-nee-tsa
a manager	**rukovoditelj**
	ruh-ckau-**vau**-dee-tely
a housewife	**kućanica**
	koo-**cha**-nee-tsa
I work from home	**Ja radim od kuće**
	ya **rah**-deem aud **koo**-cheh
I'm self-employed	**Ja sam poduzetnik**
	ya sahm pau-**doo**-zet-neeck

Weather

prognoza vremena prau-**gnau**-za **vre**-me-na	weather forecast
promjenjivo vrijeme prau-**mye**-nyee-vau vree-**ye**-me	changeable weather
vedro ved-rau	fine
loše lau-she	bad
oblačno aub-latch-nau	cloudy

It's sunny	**Sunčano je**
	soon-tcha-nau ye
It's raining	**Pada kiša**
	p**ah**-dah **kee**-sha

 > **Leisure/interests** (p 69) > **Sport** (p 74)

It's snowing	**Pada snijeg**
	pah-dah **snee**-yeg
It's windy	**Vjetrovito je**
	vye-**trau**-vee-tau ye
What a lovely day!	**Baš divan dan!**
	bash **dee**-van dahn!
What awful weather!	**Baš gadno vrijeme!**
	bash **gad**-nau vree-**ye**-me!
What will the weather be like tomorrow?	**Kakvo će vrijeme biti sutra?**
	kack-vau ch-e vree-**ye**-me **bee**-tee **soo**-trah?
Do you think it's going to rain?	**Misliš li da će biti kiše?**
	mees-leesh lee dah che **bee**-tee **kee**-she?
It's very hot/cold today	**Jako je vruće/hladno danas**
	yah-koh ye **vroo**-che/**hlah**-dnau **dah**-nas
Do you think there will be a storm?	**Misliš li da će biti oluje?**
	mees-leesh lee dah che **bee**-tee au-**loo**-ye?
Do you think it will snow?	**Mislite li da će pasti snijeg?**
	mees-lee-te lee dah che **pas**-tee **snee**-yeg?
Will it be foggy?	**Hoće li biti maglovito?**
	hau-che lee **bee**-tee mahg-**lau**-vee-tau?
What is the temperature?	**Koja je temperatura?**
	kau-ya ye tem-pe-**ra**-too-rah?

Getting around

Asking the way

nasuprot	**nah**-soop-raut	opposite
uz/pokraj	ooz/**pau**-ckray	next to
blizu	**blee**-zoo	near to
semafor	**se**-mah-faur	traffic lights
raskrsnica **ras**-krs-nee-tsa		crossroads
ugao ulice **oo**-gow **oo**-lee-tse		street corner

FACE TO FACE

A Oprostite, kako mogu doći do kolodvora?
   aup-**raus**-tee-te, **kah**-koh **mau**-goo **dau**-chee dau
      kau-lau-dvau-rah?
   Excuse me, how do I get to the station?

B Idite ravno, nah–kon crkve skrenite lijevo/
      desno!
   ee-dee-te **rah**-vnau, **nah**-kon tsr-kve **skre**-nee-te
      lee-**ye**-vau/**des**-noh!
   Keep straight on, after the church turn left/right!

26

A Je li daleko?
ye lee **dah**-le-koh?
Is it far?

B Ne, 200 metara/pet minuta
ne, **dv**-**ye**-stau **me**-tah-rah/pet mee-**noo**-tah
No, 200 yds/five minutes

A Hvala vam!
hvah-la vahm!
Thank you!

B Nema na čemu
ne-mah nah **che**-moo
You're welcome

We're lost	Mi smo zalutali
	mee smau zah-**loo**-tah-lee
We're looking for...	Mi tražimo...
	mee **trah**-zhee-moh...
Is this the right way to...?	Je li ovo pravi put do...?
	ye lee **au**v-oh **prah**-vee poot doh...?
Can I/we walk there?	Mogu li/možemo li hodati do tamo?
	mau-goo lee/**mau**-zhe-moh lee **hau**-dah-tee doh **tah**-moh?
How do I/ we get...	Kako mogu/možemo doći...
	kah-koh **mau**-goo/ **mau**-zhe-moh **dau**-chee...
onto the motorway?	do autoceste?
	doh **ow**-toh-**tse**-ste?

to the museum?	**Do muzeja?**
	doh moo-ze-ya?
to the shops?	**Do dućana?**
	doh doo-cha-nah?
Can you show me on the map?	**Možete li mi pokazati na karti?**
	mau-zhe-te lee mee **pau**-kah-**zah**-tee nah **kah-r**-tee?

YOU MAY HEAR...

Tamo dalje **tah**-moh **dah**-lye	further down
iza ee-zah	behind
onda pitajte opet **aun**-dah **pee**-tay-te au-pet	then ask again

Bus, coach and tram

In cities you buy tickets from tobacconists, kiosks and bars. You must punch them in the machine on board the bus or tram. Village buses are referred to as **autobus** or **lokalni autobus** (coach).

Is there a bus/tram to...?	**Ide li autobus/tramvaj za...?**
	ee-de lee **ow-toh**-boos/**trahm**-vay zah...?
Where do I catch the bus/tram to...?	**Gdje mogu naći autobus/tramvaj za...?**
	gdye **mau**-goo **nah**-chee **ow-toh**-boos/**trahm**-vay zah...?

A Oprostite, koji autobus vozi do centra?
aup-roh-stee-te, **koh**-yee **ow**-**toh**-boos **voh**-zee doh **tsen**-trah?
Excuse me, which bus goes to the centre?

B Broj petnaest
brauy **pet**-nah-est
Number 15

A Gdje je postaja?
gdye ye **poh**-sta-ya?
Where is the bus stop?

B Tamo, desno
tah-moh, **des**-noh
There, on the right

A Gdje mogu kupiti karte?
gdye **mau**-goo **koo**-pee-tee **kahr**-te?
Where can I buy the tickets?

B Na kiosku/trafici
nah **kee**-ohs-koo/**trah**-fee-tsee
At the news-stand/tobacconist

We're going to...	**Mi idemo u...**
	mee **ee**-demoh oo...
How much is it to go...?	**Koliko košta put...?**
	kau-lee-koh **kaush**-tah poot...?
to the centre	**do centra**
	doh **tsen**-trah
to the beach	**do plaže**
	doh **plah**-zhe

Bus, coach and tram

29

How often are the buses to...?	**Koliko često ide autobus za...?**
	kau-lee-koh **ches**-toh **ee**-de **ow**-**toh**-boos zah...?
When is the first/ the last bus to...?	**Kad je prvi/posljednji autobus za...?**
	kahd ye pr-vee/**paus**-lyed-nyee **ow**-**toh**-boos zah...?
Please tell me when to get off	**Molim vas kažite mi kad trebam sići**
	mau-leem vahs **kah**-zhee-te mee kahd **tre**-bahm **see**-chee
Please let me off	**Molim dopustite mi sići**
	mau-leem dau-**poos**-tee-te mee **s**ee-chee
This is my stop	**Ovo je moja postaja**
	au-vau ye **moy**-ah **post**-ah-ya

YOU MAY HEAR...

Ovo je vaša postaja **auv**-oh ye **vash**-ah **paus**-tah-ya	This is your stop
Uzmite taksi, to je brže **ooz**-mee-te **tah**-ksee, toh ye **br**-zhe	Take the taxi, it's quicker

Train

•••

You can buy tickets in advance of your departure date. If you are taking a fast train, check whether there is a supplement to pay.

lokalni **lau**-kahl-nee	slow train (stops at all stations)
putnički **poot**-nee-chkee	local train (stops at most stations)
ubrzani **oo**-br-zah-nee	(stops at main stations)
brzi br-zee	intercity (stops at main stations: supplement)
ekspresni **eks**-press-nee	high-speed intercity (reservations compulsory)
peron **pe**-raun	platform
blagajna **blah**-gay-nah	ticket office
vozni red **vauz**-ni red	timetable
kasni **kahs**-nee	delayed
izgubljena prtljaga iz-**gub**-lye-nah prt-**lyah**-gah	lost luggage

Where is the station?	**Gdje je kolodvor?** gd-ye ye **kau**-lau-dvaur?
one ticket	**jednu kartu** **yed**-noo **kahr**-too
two tickets	**dvije karte** **dvee**-ye **kahr**-te
to...	**do...** dau...
first/second class	**prvi/drugi razred** prvee/**droo**-gee **rahz**-red

> **Luggage** (p 90)

Getting around

A Kad je idući vlak za…?
kahd ye **ee**-doo-chee vlahk zah…?
When is the next train to…?

B U sedamnaest sati i deset minuta
oo se-**dahm**-nah-est **sah**-tee ee **des**-et mee-**noo**-ta
At 17.10

A Ja bih tri karte, molim
ya bee-h tree **kah-r**-te, **mau**-lee-m
I'd like 3 tickets, please

B U jednom smjeru ili povratne?
oo **yed**-naum **smye**-roo **ee**-lee **pauv**-raht-ne?
Single or return?

smoking/ non smoking	za pušače/za nepušače zah poo-**shah**-tche/zah **ne**-poo-**shah**-tche
Is there a supplement to pay?	Treba li platiti dodatak? **tre-bah** lee **plah**-tee-tee **dau**-dah-tack?
I want to book a seat on the fast train to Zagreb	Želim rezervirati mjesto na ekspresnom vlaku do Zagreba **zhe**-lee-m re-zer-**vee**-rah-tee **mye**-stoh nah eks-**press**-nom vlahku doh **zah**-grebah
Do I have to change?	Trebam li presjedati? **tre**-bahm lee **pre**-sye-dah-tee?
How long is there for the connection?	Koliko dugo trebam čekati na presjedanje? **kau**-lee-koh **doo**-goh **tre**-bahm **che**-kah-tee nah **pre**-sye-dah-nye?

Which platform does it leave from?	**S kojeg perona polazi vlak?** s **kau**-yeg **pe**-rau-nah **pau**-lah-zee vlahk?
Is this the train for...?	**Ide li ovaj vlak za...?** **ee**-de lee **au**-vay vlahk zah...?
Does it stop at...?	**Da li staje u...?** dah lee **stah**-ye oo...?
When does it arrive in...?	**Kad stiže u...?** kahd **stee**-zhe oo...?
Please tell me when we get to...	**Molim kažite mi kad stignemo u...** **mau**-leem **kah**-zhee-te mee kahd **stee**-gneh-moh oo...
Is there a restaurant car?	**Ima li vlak vagon–restoran?** **ee**-mah lee vlahk **vah**-gaun-res-**tau**-rahn?
Is this seat free?	**Je li ovo sjedalo slobodno?** ye lee **au**-voh **sye**-dah-loh **slau**-baud-noh?
Excuse me! (to get past)	**Molim, propustite me!** **mau**-leem, prau-**poos**-tee-te me!

Taxi

· ·

The easiest place to find a taxi stand is at a railway station. Official taxis are generally near train/bus stations or airports/ports (yellow in colour).

> **Luggage** (p 90)

I want a taxi	**Ja želim taksi**
	ya **zhe**-leem **tahk**-see
Where can I get a taxi?	**Gdje mogu naći taksi?**
	gdye **mau**-goo **nah**-chee **tahk**-see?
Please order me a taxi...	**Molim naručite mi taksi...**
	mau-leem nah-**roo**-chee-te mee **tahk**-see...
now	**sad**
	sahd
How much will it cost to go to...?	**Koliko košta vožnja do...?**
	kau-lee-koh **kaush**-tah **vauzh**-nyah doh...?
to the station	**do kolodvora**
	doh **kau**-laud-vau-rah
to the airport	**do zračne luke**
	doh **zrah**-chne **loo**-ke
to this address	**do ove adrese**
	doh **au**-ve **add**-re-se
How much is it?	**Koliko je to?**
	kau-lee-koh ye toh?
It's more than on the meter	**To je više no na taksimetru**
	toh ye **vee**-she noh nah **tahk**-see-**met**-roo
Keep the change	**Zadržite sitniš**
	zah-dr-zhee-te **seet**-neesh
Sorry, I don't have any change	**Žao mi je, nemam sitniša**
	zhow mee ye, **ne**-mahm **seet**-nee-shah

I'm in a hurry	**žurim**
	zhoo-reem
I have to catch...	**Moram stići na...**
	mau-rahm **stee**-chee nah...
a train	**vlak**
	vlahk
a plane	**zrakoplov**
	zrah-koh-plauv

Boat and ferry

You can buy travel cards in the UK which allow you to use all the ships, trains, coaches, ferries and water buses (**brodovi, vlakovi, autobusi, trajekti i gliseri**).

A ticket to Hvar for	**Jednu kartu za Hvar**
	yed-noo **kahr**-too zah hvahr
one day	**jedan dan**
	ye-dahn dahn
two days	**dva dana**
	dvah **dah**-nah
How much is it for an hour on the boat?	**Koliko košta sat vožnje brodom?**
	kau-lee-koh **kaush**-tah saht
	vauzh-nye **brau**-dohm?
Have you a timetable?	**Imate li vozni red?**
	ee-mah-te lee **vauz**-nee red?

> **Luggage** (p 90)

Is there a car ferry to...?	**Ide li trajekt za...?**
	ee-de lee **trah**-yeckt zah...?
How much is a ticket...?	**Koliko košta karta...?**
	kau-lee-koh **kaush**-tah **kahr**-tah...?
return	**povratna**
	pauv-raht-nah
single	**u jednom smjeru**
	oo **yed**-naum **smye**-roo
How much is it for a car and ... people?	**Koliko košta za auto i ... ljudi?**
	kau-lee-koh **kaush**-tah zah **ow**-toh ee ... **lyoo**-dee?
Where does the ship leave from?	**Odakle brod polazi, molim?**
	au-dahkle braud **pau**-lah-zee, **mau**-leem?
for Hvar	**Za Hvar**
	zah hvahr
When is the first/ the last boat?	**Kad je prvi/zadnji brod?**
	kahd ye **pr**-vee/**zahd**-nyee braud?

YOU MAY HEAR...

Ovo je zadnji brod au-voh ye zahd-**nyee** braud	This is the last boat
Danas ne vozi dah-nahs ne **vo**-zee **zbog prosvjeda** zbog **praus**-vyed-ah	There is no service today... because there is a strike

36

Air travel

....

dolazak **dau**-lah-zahk	arrivals
odlazak **aud**-lah-zahk	departures
međunarodni	international
me-joo-**nah**-raud-nee	
domaći **dau**-machi	domestic
ukrcajni izlaz	boarding gate
oo-kr-tzay-nee **eez**-lahz	

How do I get to the airport?	**Kako mogu doći do zračne luke?**
	kah-koh **mau**-goo **dau**-chee doh **zrach**-ne **loo**-ke?
Is there a bus to the airport?	**Ide li autobus do zračne luke?**
	ee-deh lee ow-**toh**-boos doh **zrach**-ne **loo**-ke?
Where is the luggage for the flight from...?	**Gdje je prtljaga leta iz...?**
	gdye ye **pr**-tlyah-gah **le**-tah eez...?
Where can I change some money?	**Gdje mogu promijeniti nešto novca?**
	gd-ye **mau**-goo **prau**-mee-**ye**-nee-tee **nesh**-toh **nauv**-tsah?
How do I/we get into town?	**Kako mogu/možemo doći do grada?**
	kah-koh **mau**-goo/**mau**-zhee-moh **dau**-chee doh **grah**-dah?

How much is it by taxi...	**Koliko je vožnja taksijem...** **kau**-lee-koh ye **vauzh**-nya **tahk**-see-yem...
to go into town?	**do grada?** doh **grah**-dah?
to go to the hotel...?	**do hotela...?** doh ho-**te**-la...?

YOU MAY HEAR...

Ukrcaj će biti na izlazu broj... oo-**kr**-**tsay** che **bee**-tee nah **eez**-lah-zoo brauy...	Boarding will take place at gate number...
Odmah idite do izlaza broj... **aud**-mah **ee**-dee-te doh **eez**-lah-zah brauy...	Go immediately to gate number...

Customs control

Foreign visitors do not normally require visas to enter Croatia. Visit the Croatian Ministry of Foreign Affairs' webpage to check if you require a visa (www.mvpei.hr).

> **Luggage** (p 90)

putovnica poo-**tauv**-nee-tsah	passport
osobne iskaznice **au**-saub-ne **ees**-kahz-nee-tse	identity cards
carina **tsah**-ree-nah	customs

Do I have to pay duty on this?	**Trebam li platiti carinu za ovo?** **tre**-bahm lee **plah**-tee-tee **tsah**-ree-nooh zah **auv**-oh?
It's for my own personal use/ for a present	**To je za moju osobnu uporabu/poklon** toh ye zah **mau**-yoo **aus**-aub-noo **oo**-poh-rah-boo/**pau**-klaun
We are on our way to ... (if in transit through a country)	**Mi smo na proputovanju za ...** mee smoh nah **prau**-poo-tau-**vah**-nyoo zah...
The child is/ children are on this passport	**Dijete je/Djeca su na ovoj putovnici** **dee**-ye-te ye/**dy-e**-tsa soo nah **au**-vohy poo-**tauv**-nee-tsee

39

Driving

Car hire

vozačka dozvola vau-**zatch**-kah **dauz**-vau-lah	driving licence
puno kasko osiguranje **poo**-noh **kah**-skoh **aus**-ee-goo-**rah**-nye	fully comprehensive insurance

I want to hire a car	**Želim unajmiti auto** zhe-leem oo-**ny**-mee-tee **ow**-toh
for ... days	**na ... dana** nah ... **dah**-nah
with automatic gears	**s automatskim mjenjačem** s **ow**-toh-**maht**-skeem mye-**nya**-tchem
What are your rates...?	**Koje su vaše cijene...?** k**oh**-ye soo vashe tsee-**ye**-ne...?
per day	**dnevno** **dneh**-vnoh
per week	**tjedno** **ty**-**e**-dnoh
How much is the deposit?	**Koliko je polog?** **kau**-lee-koh ye **pau**-laug?

40

Do you take credit cards?	**Primate li kreditne kartice?**
	pree-mah-te lee **kre**-deet-ne **kahr**-tee-tse?
Is there a mileage (kilometre) charge?	**Ima li naplata po kilometru?**
	ee-mah lee **nah**-plah-tah pau **kee**-lau-me-troo?
How much is it?	**Koliko je to?**
	kau-lee-koh ye toh?
Does the price include fully comprehensive insurance?	**Je li u cijenu uračunato puno kasko osiguranje?**
	ye lee oo tsee-**ye**-noo **oo**-rah-**tchu**-nah-toh **poo**-noh **kah**-sko **aus**-ee-goo-**rah**-ny-e?
Must I return the car here?	**Moram li vratiti auto ovdje?**
	maur-ahm lee **vrah**-tee-tee **ow**-toh **auv**-dyeh?
By what time?	**Do koliko sati?**
	doh **kau**-lee-koh sah-tee?
I'd like to leave it in... (masc.)/(fem.)	**Ja bih ostavio/ostavila auto u...**
	ya beeh **aus**-tah-veo/ **aus**-tah-vee-lah **ow**-toh oo...

Car hire

YOU MAY HEAR...

Molim vratite auto s punim rezervoarom	Please return the car with a full tank
maul-eem **vrah**-tee-te **ow**-toh s **poo**-neem **re**-zer-voh-**ah**-rom	

41

Driving and petrol

The speed limits in Croatia are 40 km/h in built up areas, 60–90 km/h on main roads, 100 km/h on 2-lane motorways and 120 km/h on 3-lane motorways (except in bad weather and at night). Drivers are required to keep their headlights on in the daytime.

Driving

Can I/we park here?	**Mogu li/možemo li ovdje parkirati?** **mau**-goo lee/**mau**-zhee-moh lee **auv**-dyeh pah-r-**kee**-rah-tee?
How long for?	**Koliko dugo?** **kau**-lee-koh **doo**-goh?
Which junction is it for...?	**Za koje pravce je ova raskrsnica?** zah **kau**-ye **prahv**-tse ye au-vah **rahsk**-r-snee-tsah?
Do I/we need snow chains?	**Trebam li/trebamo li lance za snijeg?** **tre**-bahm lee/**tre**-bah-moh lee **lahn**-tse zah **snee**-yeg?

Many petrol stations are now self-service and you can pay by inserting your card or a banknote into the appropriate slot on the pump.

super **soo**-per	4 star
dizel **dee**-zel	diesel
bezolovni	unleaded
bez-au-lauv-nee	

Fill it up, please	Napunite, molim
	nah-poo-nee-te, **mau**-leem
Please check the oil/the water	Molim, provjerite ulje/vodu
	mau-leem, **prauv**-ye-ree-te **oo**-lye/**vau**-doo
30 euros worth of unleaded petrol	Bezolovnog goriva za trideset eura
	bez-**au**-lauv-nog **gaur**-ee-vah zah **tree**-de-set e-**oo**-rah
Where is...?	Gdje je...?
	gdye ye...?
the air line	dovod zraka
	doh-vaud **zrah**-kah
water	vode
	vau-de
pump number...	broj pumpe...
	broh-y p**oom**-pe
Where do I pay?	Gdje mogu platiti?
	gd-ye mau-goo **plah**-tee-tee?
Can I pay by credit card?	Mogu li platiti kreditnom karticom?
	mau-goo lee **plah**-tee-tee **kre**-deet-naum **kahr**-tee-tsaum?

Breakdown

If you break down, the emergency phone number for the Croatian equivalent to the AA (Hrvatski Auto Klub — HAK), Pomoć na cesti **pau**-mauch nah **tse**-stee is 987 or +3851987 from a mobile. Garages that do repairs are known as automehaničarske radionice (auto-mechanics) or popravke vozila (car repairs).

Can you help me?	Možete li mi pomoći? **mau**-zhe-te lee mee **pau**-mau-chee?
My car has broken down	Moj auto je u kvaru mauy **ow**-toh ye oo **kvah**-roo
I've run out of petrol	Nestalo mi je goriva **ne**-stah-lau mee ye **gau**-ree-vah
Can you tow me to the nearest garage?	Možete li me odvući do najbliže pumpe? **mau**-zhe-te lee me **aud**-voo-chee doh **nay**-blee-zhe **poom**-pe?

Driving

Do you have parts for a (make of car)...?	**Imate li dijelove za...?** **ee**-mah-te lee dee-**ye**-lau-ve...?
There's something wrong with the...	**Nešto nije u redu s/sa...** **nesh**-toh **nee**-ye oo **re**-doo s/sah...
Can you replace...?	**Možete li zamijeniti...?** **mau**-zhe-te lee **zah**-mee-ye-nee-tee...?

Car parts

• •

| The ... doesn't work | ... **ne radi** ... ne **rah**-dee |
| The ... don't work | ... **ne rade** ... ne **rah**-de |

accelerator	gas	gahs
alternator	alternator	al-**ter**-nah-tor
battery	akumulator	**ah**-koo-moo-**lah**-taur
bonnet	poklopac	**pauk**-lau-pats
brakes	kočnice	**kautch**-nee-tse
choke	čok	tchok
clutch	spojka	**spoy**-kah
distributor	pogonsko vratilo	**pau**-gaun-skoh **vrah**-tee-loh
engine	motor	**mau**-taur
exhaust	ispušna cijev	**ees**-poosh-nah **tsee**-yev

fuse	osigurač	au-see-**goo**-rahtch
gears	brzine	br-**zee**-ne
handbrake	ručna kočnica	**rootch**-nah **kotch**-nee-tsa
headlights	prednja svjetla	**pred**-nyah **svye**-tlah
ignition	paljenje	**pah**-lye-nye
indicator	pokazivač smjera	**pau**-kah-**zee**-vatch **smye**-rah
points	pogonski motor	**pau**-gaun-skee **mau**-taur
radiator	hladnjak	**hlahd**-nyack
reverse gear	vožnja unatrag	**vozh**-nya oo-**nah**-trag
seat belt	pojas	**pau**-yahs
spark plug	svjećica	**svye-chee**-tsah
steering	upravljač	**oop**-rahv-**lya**-tchah
steering wheel	upravljački prigon	**oop**-rahv-lyatch-kee **pree**-gaun
tyre	profil gume	**prau**-feel **goo**-me
wheel	kotač	**kau**-tatch
windscreen	vjetrobran	**vye**-trav-brahn
windscreen washer	perač vjetrobrana	**peh**-ratch **vye**-trau-brahna
windscreen wiper	brisač	**bree**-sahch

46

Road signs

Road signs	Prometni znakovi
Motorway signs	Znakovi za autocestu
Road network	Cestovna mreža
Road map	Autokarta
North	Sjever
South	Jug
West	Zapad
East	Istok
Detour	Zaobilaznica
Toll	Cestarina
Right	Desno
Left	Lijevo

Motorway	Autocesta
Fast traffic road	Brza cesta
State road	Državna cesta
Regional road	Županijska cesta
Local road	Lokalna cesta
Maximum speed	Maksimalna brzina
Dangerous bend	Opasna okuka/zavoj
Warning	Oprez
Drive slowly	Vozi polako
Pedestrians	Pješaci
No parking	Zabranjeno parkiranje
Road works	Radovi na cesti
All vehicles prohibited	Zabranjeno svim vozilima

Staying somewhere

Hotel (booking)

● ●

Bed and breakfasts, particularly on farms and
in the countryside, are becoming very popular.
You can find out more about **turizam** (tourism)
on **www.croatia.hr**

jednokrevetna soba	single room
dvokrevetna soba	double room
vlastita kupaonica	private facilities
broj odraslih	number of adults
broj djece	number of children

Do you have a room for tonight?	**Imate li sobu za noćas?**
	ee-mah-te lee **sau**-boo zah **nau**-chahs?
with bath	**s kupaonicom**
	s koo-**pah**-oh-nee-tsaum
with shower	**s tušem**
	s **too**-shehm
with a double bed	**s bračnim krevetom**
	s **bra**-tch-neem **kre**-ve-taum

49

FACE TO FACE

A Ja bih rezervirala (fem.)/**rezervirao** (masc.)
ya beeh re-zer-**vee**-rah-lah/re-zer-**vee**-row
I'd like to book

jednokrevetnu/**dvokrevetnu sobu**
ye-dnau-**kre**-vet-noo/**dvau-kre**-vet-noo **sau**-boo
a single/double room

B Koliko noći?
k**au**-lee-koh **nau**-chee?
How many nights?

A Jednu noć/... noći/od ... do ...
zah **yed**-noo nauch/... **nau**-chee/aud ... doh ...
for one night/... nights/from ... till ...

Koliko je jedna noć/jedan tjedan?
k**au**-lee-koh ye **ye**-dnah nauch/**ye**-dahn **ty**e-dahn?
How much is it per night/per week?

with twin beds	**s dva kreveta**
	s **dva kre**-vetah
with an extra bed for a child	**s krevetom za dijete**
	s **kre**-ve-taum zah dee-**ye**-te
Is breakfast included?	**Da li je zajutrak uračunat?**
	da lee ye **zah**-yoot-rack **oo**-rah-**choo**-naht?
Have you anything cheaper?	**Imate li išta jeftinije?**
	ee-mah-te lee **ee**-shtah yef-**tee**-nee-ye?
I'd like to see the room	**Mogu li vidjeti sobu?**
	mau-goo lee **vee**-dye-tee s**au**-boo

Puni smo	**poo**-nee smoh	We're full
Vaše ime, molim		Your name, please
vah-she **ee**-me, **mau**-leem		
Molim, potvrdite...		Please confirm...
maul-eem, **pau-t**v-r-dee-te...		
e-mailom	ee-mail-ohm	by e-mail
faksom	fa-ksaum	by fax

Hotel (desk)

•••••••••••••••••••••••••••••••••••••

Many hotels are now signposted in towns. The Croatian word for hotel is **hotel**.

I booked a room... (masc.)/(fem.)	**Rezervirao/rezervirala sam sobu...**
	re-zer-**vee**-row/**re**-zer-**vee**-rah-lah sahm **sau**-boo...
in the name of...	**na ime...**
	nah **ee**-me...
Where can I park the car?	**Gdje mogu parkirati auto?**
	gd-ye **mau**-goo **pahr**-kee-**rah**-tee **ow**-toh?
What time is...?	**Kad je...?**
	kahd ye...?
dinner	**večera**
	ve-che-rah

breakfast	**zajutrak**
	zah-yoo-track
lunch	**ručak**
	roo-tchack
The key, please	**Ključ, molim**
	klyootch, **mau**-leem
Room number...	**Broj sobe...**
	brauy **sau**-be...
Are there any messages for me?	**Ima li poruka za mene?**
	ee-mah lee **pau**-roo-kah zah **me**-ne?
Can I send a fax?	**Mogu li poslati faks?**
	mau-goo lee **paus**-lah-tee fa-ks?
I'm leaving tomorrow	**Odlazim sutra**
	aud-lah-zeem **soo**-trah
Please prepare the bill	**Molim, pripremite račun**
	mau-leem, **pree**-pre-mee-te **ra**-tchoon

Camping

●●●

otpatci **aut**-pah-tse	rubbish
pitka voda **peet**-kah **vau**-dah	drinking water
priključak za struju **pri**-klyu-tchak zah str-**oo**-yoo	electric point

Is there a restaurant in the camp?	**Ima li u kampu restoran?** **ee**-mah lee oo **kahm**-poo res-**tau**-rahn?
Do you have any vacancies?	**Imate li slobodnih mjesta?** **ee**-mah-te lee **slau**-baud-neeh **mye**s-tah?
How much is it per night?	**Koliko košta noć?** **kau**-lee-koh **kaush**-tah nauch?
per tent	**za šator** zah **sha**-taur
per caravan	**za prikolicu** zah **pree**-kau-lee-tsoo
per person	**po osobi** poh **aus**-au-bee
Does the price include...?	**Da li cijena uključuje...?** **dah** lee tsee-**ye**-nah **oo**-klyu-t**choo**-yeh...?
showers	**tuševe** **too**-she-ve
hot water	**toplu vodu** **taup**-loo **vau**-doo
electricity	**struju** **stroo**-yoo
We'd like to stay for ... nights	**Mi bismo boravili ... noći** mee **bee**-smoh **bau**-rah-vee-lee ... **nau**-chee

Self-catering

Who do we contact if there are problems?	**Koga možemo kontaktirati ako bude problema?**
	kau-gah **mau**-zhe-mo **kaun**-tahk-**tee**-rah-tee **ah**-koh **boo**-de **praub**-le-mah?
How does the heating work?	**Kako radi grijanje?**
	kah-koh **rah**-dee **gree**-yah-ny-e?
Is there always hot water?	**Ima li uvijek tople vode?**
	ee-mah lee oo-**vee**-yek **taup**-le **vau**-de?
Where is the nearest supermarket?	**Gdje je najbliže samoposluživanje?**
	gdye ye **nay**-blee-zhah **sah**-moh-**paus**-loo-jee-vah-nye?
Where do we leave the rubbish?	**Gdje se odlaže otpatke?**
	gdye se **aud**-lah-zhe **aut**-paht-ke?

> **Sightseeing and tourist office** (p 67)

Shopping

Shopping phrases
• •

Opening hours are approx. 8.30 am to 12.30 pm
and 4 to 7.30 pm Mon. to Sat. Opening hours tend
to be longer in summer. Some supermarkets
(**samoposluge**) are open all day.

FACE TO FACE

A Što želite?/Izvolite, što biste htjeli?
  shtoh **zhe**-lee-te?/**eez**-vau-lee-te, shtoh **bees**-te
  htye-lee?
  What would you like?

B Imate li...?
  ee-mah-te lee...?
  Do you have...?

A Sigurno, izvolite. Još nešto?
  see-goor-noh, **eez**-vaul-lee-te. yaush **nesh**-toh?
  Certainly, here you are. Anything else?

Where is...?	**Gdje je...?**
	gdye ye...?
I'm just looking	**Samo gledam**
	sah-moh **gle**-dahm
I'm looking for a present for...	**Ja tražim poklon za...**
	ya **trah**-jeem **pau**k-laun zah...
my mother	**svoju majku**
	svau-yoo **may**-koo
a child	**dijete**
	dee-ye-te
Where can I buy...?	**Gdje mogu kupiti...?**
	gd-ye **mau**-goo **koo**-pee-tee...?
shoes	**cipele**
	tsee-pe-le
gifts	**poklone**
	pauk-lau-ne
Do you have anything...?	**Imate li išta...?**
	ee-mah-te lee **eesh**-tah...?
larger	**veće**
	ve-che
smaller	**manje**
	mah-nye
It's too expensive for me	**To mi je preskupo**
	toh mee ye **pres**-koo-poh
Can you give me a discount?	**Mogu li dobiti popust?**
	mau-goo lee **dau**-bee-tee **pau**-poost?

56

Shops

rasprodaja **rahs**-prau-dah-yah	sale
popust **pau**-poost	discount
zatvoreno za blagdane zah-**tvau**-re-noh zah **blah**-g-dah-ne	closed for holidays

baker's	Pekarnica	**peck**-ahr-nee-tsah
butcher's	Mesnica	**mes**-nee-tsah
cake shop	Slastičarna	**slah**-stee-chahr-nah
clothes	Odjeća	**aud**-ye-chah
fruit shop	Voćarna	**vau**-chahr-nah
gifts	Pokloni/ Suveniri	**pauk**-laun-ee/ **soo**-ve-nee-ree
grocer's	Mješovita roba	mye-**shoh**-vee-tah **rau**-bah
hairdresser's	Frizer/ Brijačnica	fr**ee**-zer/bree-**yach**-nee-tsah
newsagent	Novine/ Kiosk	**nauv**-ee-ne/ **trah**-phee-kah
optician	Optičar	**aup**-tee-tchahr
perfume shop	Parfumerija	pahr-phoo-**me**-ree-yah
pharmacy	Ljekarna	l**ye**-kahr-nah
photographic shop	Fotograf	f**au**-taug-rahph

57

shoe shop	**Obuća**	**au**-boo-chah
sports shop	**Športska**	**shpaurt**-skah
	odjeća	**aud**-ye-chah
supermarket	**Samoposluga**	sah-moh-**paus**-
		loo-gah
tobacconist's	**Duhan**	**doo**-hahn
toys	**Igračke**	**eeg**-rahch-ke

Food (general)

biscuit	**keks**	kecks
bread	**kruh**	kroo-h
bread roll	**pecivo**	**pe**-tsee-voh
bread (brown)	**crni kruh**	**cr**-nee kroo-h
butter	**maslac**	**mah**-slahts
cheese	**sir**	seer
chicken	**piletina**	**pee**-le-tee-nah
coffee (instant)	**instant kava**	**een**-stahnt kah-vah
cream	**vrhnje**	vr-h-nye
crisps	**čips**	chips
eggs	**jaja**	yah-yah
fish	**riba**	ree-bah
ham (cooked)	**kuhana**	**koo**-hah-nah
	šunka	**shoon**-kah
ham (cured)	**pršut**	pr-shoot
herbal tea	**biljni čaj**	**beely**-nee tchay
jam	**džem**	jem

juice, orange	**narančada**	**nah**-rahn-**chah**-dah
margarine	**margarin**	mahr-**gah**-reen
marmalade	**marmelada**	mahr-me-**lah**-dah
milk	**mlijeko**	mlee-**ye**-koh
olive oil	**maslinovo ulje**	**mahs**-lee-nau-voh **oo**-lye
pepper	**papar**	**pah**-pahr
salt	**sol**	saul
sugar	**šećer**	**she**-cher
tea	**čaj**	tchay
tomatoes (tin)	**limenka rajčica**	**lee**-men-kah **ray**-chee-tsah
vinegar	**ocat**	**au**-tsaht
yoghurt	**jogurt**	**yaug**-oort

Food (fruit and veg)

Fruit **voće** vau-che

apples	**jabuke**	**yah**-boo-ke
apricots	**marelice**	**mah**-re-lee-tse
bananas	**banane**	**bah**-nah-ne
cherries	**trešnje**	**tresh**-nye
grapefruit	**grejpfrut**	**greyp**-froot
grapes	**grožđe**	**grauzh**-je
lemon	**limun**	**lee**-moon
melon	**dinja**	**dee**-nya

oranges	**naranče**	**nah**-rahn-tche
peaches	**breskve**	**bres**-kve
pears	**kruške**	**kroosh**-ke
plums	**šljive**	**shlyee**-ve
raspberries	**maline**	**mah**-lee-ne
strawberries	**jagode**	**ya**-gau-de
watermelon	**lubenica**	loo-**ben**-ee-tsah

Vegetables **povrće pau**-vr-che

asparagus	**šparoge**	**shpah**-rau-ge
aubergine	**patlidžan**	**paht**-lee-jahn
carrots	**mrkve**	mr-kve
cauliflower	**cvjetača**	**tsvye**-tah-chah
celery	**celer**	**tse**-ler
cucumber	**krastavac**	**krah**-stah-vahts
garlic	**češnjak**	**chesh**-nyahk
leek	**poriluk**	**pau**-ree-look
mushrooms	**gljive**	**glyee**-ve
onions	**luk**	look
peas	**grašak**	**grah**-shack
pepper	**paprika**	**pah**-pree-kah
potatoes	**krumpiri**	**kroom**-pee-ree
runner beans	**mahune**	**mah**-hoo-ne
salad	**salata**	**sah**-lah-tah
spinach	**špinat**	**shpee**-nat
tomatoes	**rajčice**	**ray**-tchee-tse

Clothes

··

women's sizes		men's suit sizes		shoe sizes			
UK	EU	UK	EU	UK	EU	UK	EU
8	36	36	46	2	35	7	41
10	38	38	48	3	36	8	42
12	40	40	50	4	37	9	43
14	42	42	52	5	38	10	44
16	44	44	54	6	39	11	45
18	46	46	56				

FACE TO FACE

A **Mogu li probati ovo?**
mau-goo lee **prau**-bah-tee oh-voh?
May I try this on?

B **Molim, izvolite ovuda**
mau-leem, **eez**-vaul-lee-te au-**voo**-dah
Please come this way

A **Imate li malen/srednji/velik broj?**
ee-mah-te lee **mah**-len/**sred**-nyee/**ve**-lee-k brauy?
Do you have a small/medium/large size?

B **Koji broj nosite?**
kau-yee brauy **nau**-see-te?
What size (clothes) do you take?

Clothes

61

bigger	veće	**ve**-che
smaller	manje	**mah**-nye
in other colours	u drugoj boji	oo **droo**-gauy **bau**-yee

YOU MAY HEAR...

Koji broj cipela nosite? **kau**-yee brauy **tsee**-pe-lah **nau**-see-te?	What shoe size do you take?
U ovoj boji samo imamo ovaj broj oo **auv**-auy **bau**-yee **sah**-moh **ee**-mah-moh **auv**-y brauy	In this colour we only have this size

Clothes (articles)

blouse	bluza	**bloo**-zah
coat	kaput	**kah**-poot
dress	haljina	**hah**-lyee-nah
jacket	jakna	**yack**-nah
jumper	džemper	**jem**-per
knickers	ženske hlače	**zhen**-ske **hlah**-tche
skirt	suknja	**sook**-nyah

shorts	kratke hlače	**kraht**-ke **hlah**-tche
shirt	košulja	**kaus**-hoo-lyah
socks	čarape	**chah**-rah-pe
swimsuit	kupaći	**koo**-pah-chee
	kostim	**kaus**-teem
t-shirt	majica	**mah**-yee-tsah
trousers	hlače	**hlah**-tche

Maps and guides

kiosk **kee**-ausk	kiosk
tjedni časopis **tyed**-nee **chah**-sau-pees	a weekly magazine
novine **nau**-vee-ne	newspaper

Do you have...?	Imate li...?
	ee-mah-te lee...?
of the town	plan grada
	plahn **grah**-dah
map of the region	kartu regije
	kahr-too **reg**-ee-ye
Can you show me where ... is on the map?	Možete li mi pokazati gdje je ... na karti?
	mau-zhe-te lee mee **pau**-kah-zah-tee gd-ye ye ... nah **kahr**-tee?

63

Do you have a guidebook/ a leaflet in English?	imate li vodič/listak na engleskom?
	ee-mah-te lee **vaud**-eech/ **lees**-tak nah eng-**les**-kaum?
Do you have any English newspapers/ books?	Imate li engleske novine/ knjige?
	ee-mah-te lee eng-**les**-ke **nauv**-ee-ne?

Post office

• •

Post offices are open from approx. 7 am to either 11 am or 2 or 4 pm in smaller towns, to 7 or 8 pm in larger towns, Mon. to Fri. (they are either shut, or open from approx. 8.30 am to 2 pm, sometimes later, on Sat). For a quicker service ask for **preporučeno** or **hitno**. A postbox is marked as **poštanski sandučić**.

| Pošta | **posh**-tah | post office |
| marke | **mahr**-ke | stamps |

 > Asking the way (p 26) **> Sightseeing** (p 67)

Where is the post office?	**Gdje je pošta?** gdye ye **posh**-tah?
When does it open?	**Kada se otvara?** kahda se **au**-tva-kah?
Which is the counter...?	**Koji je šalter...?** **kau**-yee ye **shahl**-ter...?
for stamps	**za marke** zah **mahr**-ke
for parcels	**za pakete** zah **pack**-ete
six stamps for postcards...	**Šest maraka za razglednice...** shest **mah**-rah-kah zah **rahz**-gled-nee-tse...
priority post	**preporučeno** pre-**pau**-roo-che-noh
for Britain	**za Britaniju** zah **bree**-tah-nee-yoo
for America	**za Ameriku** zah **ah**-me-**ree**-koo
for Australia	**za Australiju** zah ows-**trah**-lee-yoo

YOU MAY HEAR...

Marke možete kupiti na kiosku **mahr**-ke **mau**-zhe-te **koo**-pee-tee nah **kee**-aus-koo	You can buy stamps at the kiosk

> **Money** (p 87) > **Paying** (p 88)

Photos

● ●

Film can be bought from kiosks, in photographic shops, gift shops or supermarkets, but usually not in pharmacies.

A tape for this camcorder	**Kazetu za ovu kameru** kah-ze-tu zah **auv**-oo **kah**-me-roo
Do you have batteries for this camera?	**Imate li baterije za ovu kameru?** **ee**-mah-te lee bah-**te**-ree-ye zah **auv**-oo **kah**-me-roo?

Leisure

Sightseeing and tourist office

The tourist office is officially called **Turistički Ured**.
If you are looking for somewhere to stay, they will have
details of hotels, private accommodation, campsites,
etc. Most museums are closed on Sundays.

Where is the tourist office, please?	**Molim vas, gdje je turistički ured?**
	maul-eem vas, gdye ye too-**rees**-tee-chkee **oo**-red?
What can we visit in the area?	**Što možemo razgledati u ovom kraju?**
	shtau **mau**-zhe-moh rahz-**gle**-dah-tee oo **auv**-aum **krah**-yu?
in two hours	**u dva sata**
	oo dvah **sah**-tah
Have you any leaflets?	**Imate li neki turistički listak?**
	ee-mah-te lee **ne**-kee too-**rees**-teech-kee **lees**-tak?
Are there any excursions?	**Ima li neki izlet?**
	ee-mah lee **ne**-kee **eez**-let?

We'd like to go to....	**Mi bismo išli u...**
	mee **bees**-moh **eesh**-lee oo...
How much does it cost to get in?	**Koliko košta ulaz...?**
	kau-lee-koh **kaush**-tah **oo**-laz...?
Are there reductions for...?	**Imate li popust za...?**
	ee-mah-teh lee **pau**-poost zah...?
children	**djecu**
	dye-tsu
students	**studente**
	stoo-den-te
over 6os	**umirovljene**
	oo-**mee**-rauv-lye-ne

Entertainment

....

What is there to do in the evenings?	**Ima li što za razonodu navečer?**
	ee-mah lee shtoh zah rah-**zoh**-noh-doo **nah**-ve-cher?
Do you have a programme of events?	**Imate li program?**
	ee-mah-te lee **prau**-grahm?
Is there anything for children?	**Ima li sadržaja za djecu?**
	ee-mah lee sah-dr-zha-ya zah **dye**-tsoo?

Leisure/interests

. . . .

Where can I/ we go...?	**Gdje mogu/možemo ići...?** gd-ye **mau**-goo/**mau**-zhe-moh **ee**-chee...?
fishing	**ribariti** ree-**bah**-ree-tee
walking	**šetati** she-tah-tee
Are there any good beaches near here?	**Ima li u blizini dobrih plaža?** **ee**-mah lee oo **blee**-zee-nee **dau**b-reeh **plah**-jah?
Is there a swimming pool?	**Ima li bazen?** **ee**-mah lee **bah**-zen?

Music

. . . .

Are there any good concerts on?	**Ima li kakvih dobrih koncerata?** **ee**-mah lee **kah**-kveeh **dau**-breeh kaun-tse-**rah**-tah?
Where can I get tickets for the concert?	**Gdje mogu kupiti ulaznice za koncert?** gd-ye **mau**-goo **koo**-pee-tee **oo**-lahz-nee-tsoo zah **kaun**-tsert?

| Where can we hear some classical music/jazz? | Gdje možemo slušati ozbiljnu glazbu/džez? |
| | gd-ye **mau**-je-moh **sloo**-shah-tee **auz**-beely-noo **glahz**-boo/jahz? |

Cinema

....

What's on at the cinema…?	Što se prikazuje u kinu…?
	shtoh se pree/**kah**/zoo-ye oo **kee**-noo…?
What time does the film start?	Kad počinje film?
	kahd **pau**-chee-nye feelm?
How much are the tickets?	Koliko košta ulaznica?
	kau-lee-koh **kaush**-tah **oo**-lazh-nee-tsah?
Two for the (give time of perfomance) showing	Dvije za … za film…
	dvee-ye zah … za pheelm…

> **Making friends** (p 21)

Leisure

Theatre/opera

parket	**par**-ket	stalls
galerija	**gah**-le-ree-ya	circle
balkon	**bahl**-kaun	box
sjedalo	**sye**-dah-loh	seat
garderoba		cloakroom
gahr-de-rau-bah		

What is on at the theatre?	Što se daje u kazalištu? shtoh se **dah**-ye oo **kah**-zah-leesh-too?
What prices are the tickets?	Koje su cijene ulaznica? **kau**-ye soo **tsee**-ye-ne **oo**-lahz-nee-tsah?
I'd like two tickets...	Ja bih dvije ulaznice... ya beeh **dvee**-ye **oo**-lahz-nee-tse...
for tonight	za večeras zah **ve**-che-rahs
for tomorrow night	za sutra navečer zah **soot**-rah **nah**-ve-cher
for the 3rd of August	za treći kolovoza zah **tre**-chee **kau**-lau-vau-zah
When does the performance begin/end?	Kad počinje/završava predstava? kahd **pau**-chee-nye/zah-**vr**-sha-vah **pred**-stah-vah?

Ne možete ući, predstava je počela ne **mau**-zhe-te **oo**-chee, **pred**-stah-vah ye **pau**-che-lah	You can't go in, the performance has started
Možete ući za pauze **mau**-zhe-te **oo**-chee zah **pah**-oo-ze	You may enter at the interval

Television

daljinski upravljač **dah**-lyeen-skee oop-**rahv**-lyach	remote control
uključiti . **ook**-lyoo-chee-tee	to switch on
isključiti **eesk**-lyoo-chee-tee	to switch off
serija **ser**-ee-ya	series
tv sapunica tv **sah**-poo-nee-tsah	soap
dnevnik/vijesti **dnev**-neeck/vee-**yes**-tee	news
animirani film **ah**-nee-**mee**-rah-nee feelm	cartoon

Where is the television?	**Gdje je televizor?** gdye ye te-le-**vee**-zaur?
How do you switch it on?	**Kako se uključuje?** **kah**-koh vee **ook**-lyoo-tchoo-ye?
What is on television?	**Što ima na televiziji?** shtoh **ee**-mah nah te-le-**vee**-zee-yee?
When is the news?	**Kad su vijesti?** kahd soo vee-**yes**-tee?
Do you have any English-language channels?	**Imate li neki program na engleskom?** **ee**-mah-te lee **neck**-ee **praug**-rahm nah eng-**les**-kaum?
Do you have any programmes for children?	**Imate li neki program za djecu?** **ee**-mah-te lee **neck**-ee **praug**-rahm zah **dye**-tsoo?
Do you have any English videos?	**Imate li neku video kazetu na engleskom?** **ee**-mah-te lee **neck**-oo **vee**-deh-oh kah-**ze**-too nah eng-**les**-kaum?

Sport

....

Where can I/ we play...?	**Gdje mogu/možemo igrati...?**
	gdye **mau**-goo/možemo **eeg**-rah-tee...?
Where can I/ we go...?	**Gdje mogu/možemo ići...?**
	gdye **mau**-goo/**mau**-zhe-moh **ee**-chee...?
swimming	**plivati**
	plee-vah-tee
jogging	**trčati**
	tr-t**chah**-tee
Do you have to be a member?	**Moram li biti član?**
	mau-rahm li **bee**-tee t**ch**lahn?
How much is it per hour?	**Koliko košta jedan sat?**
	kau-lee-koh **kau**-shtah **ye**-dahn saht?
Can we hire...?	**Možemo li unajmiti...?**
	mau-zhe-moh lee **oo**-nay-mee-tee...?
rackets	**Rekete**
	re-cke-te
golf clubs	**golf palice**
	golf **pah**-lee-tse
We'd like to see (name team) play	**Mi bismo gledali ... utakmicu**
	mee **bee**-smoh **gle**-dah-lee ... **oo**-tahk-mee-tsoo

Where can I/ we get tickets for the game?	**Gdje mogu/možemo kupiti ulaznice za utakmicu?** gd-ye ya **mau**-goo/ mee **mau**-he-moh **koo**-pee-tee **oo**-lahz-nee-tse zah **oo**-tak-mee-tsoo?

Skiing

skijanje kroz prirodu **skee**-ya-nye krauz **pree**-rau-doo	cross-country skiing
skijaška propusnica **skee**-ya-shkah **prau**-poos-nee-tsah	ski pass

I want to hire skis	**Želim unajmiti skije**
	zhe-leem oo-**nay**-mee-tee **skee**-ye
Does the price include...?	Da li su u cijenu uračunate...?
	dah lee soo oo tsee-**yenn**-oo **oo**-rah-choo-nah-te...?
boots	čizme
	chee-zme
poles	štapovi
	shtah-pau-vee
How much is a pass...?	Koliko je propusnica...?
	kau-lee-koh ye **prau**-poos-nee-tsah...?
daily	dnevna
	dnev-nah
weekly	tjedna
	tyed-nah
When is the last ascent?	Kad je zadnji uspon?
	kahd ye **zahd**-nyee **oos**-paun?
Can you adjust my bindings?	Možete li mi podesiti vezove?
	mau-zhe-te lee mee **pau**-des-ee-tee **ve**-zoh-ve?

Jeste li ikad skijali ranije? **yes**-te lee **ee**-kahd **skee**-ya-lee **rah**-nee-ye?	Have you ever skied before?
Koju dužinu skija želite? **kau**-yoo **doo**-zhee-noo **skee**-yah **zhe**-lee-te?	What length skis do you want?
Koji broj čizama nosite? **kau**-yee brauy **chee**-zah-mah nau-see-teh?	What is your boot size?
Želite li skijašku poduku? **zhe**-lee-te lee **skee**-yash-koo **pau**-doo-koo?	Do you want skiing lessons?

Walking

....

Are there any guided walks?	Ima li kakvih šetnji s vodičem? **ee**-mah lee **kah**-kveeh **shet**-nyee s **vo**-dee-chem?
Do you know any good walks?	Znate li koju dobru šetnju? **znah**-te lee koyu **daub**-roo **shet**-nyoo?

How many kilometres is the walk?	Koliko kilometara je šetnja?
	kau-lee-koh **kee**-loh-me-tah-rah ye **shet**-nya?
Is it very steep?	Da li je vrlo strmo?
	da lee ye **vr**-loh **str**-moh?
How long will it take?	Koliko dugo će trajati?
	kau-lee-koh **doo**-goh che **trah**-ya-tee?
Is there a map of the walk?	Imate li kartu za šetnju?
	ee-mah-te lee k**ahr**-too za **shet**-nyoo?
We'd like to go climbing	Mi bismo išli planinariti
	mee **bee**-smoh eesh-lee **plah**-nee-nah-**ree**-tee
Do you have a detailed map of the area?	Imate li preciznu kartu područja?
	ee-mah-te lee **pre**-tseez-noo **kahr**-too **pod**-roo-tch-ya?

Leisure

> **Maps and guides** (p 63)

Communications

Telephone and mobile

The international code for Croatia is **oo 385** plus the Croatian town or area code less the first 0, e.g., Split (21), Šibenik (22), Zadar (23), Dubrovnik (20), etc.

telefonski broj te-le-**faun**-skee brauy	telephone number
telefonska kartica te-le-**faun**-skah **kah**r-tee-tsah	phonecard
mobilni telefon **mau**-beel-nee **te**-le-phaun	mobile

I want to make a phone call	**Želim telefonirati** **zhe**-leem te-le-**fau**-nee-rah-tee
Where can I buy a phonecard?	**Gdje mogu kupiti telefonsku karticu?** gdye **mau**-goo **koo**-pee-tee te-le-f**aun**-skoo **kahr**-tee-tsoo?

A phonecard for ... euro	**Karticu za ... eura**
	kahr-tee-tsah zah ... **e**-oo-roh
Do you have a mobile?	**Imate li mobilni?**
	ee-mah-te lee **mau**-beel-nee?
What is the number of your mobile?	**Koji je broj vašeg mobilnog telefona?**
	kau-yee ye brauy vasheg **mau**-beel-naug **te**-le-f**au**-nah?
My mobile number is...	**Broj mog telefona je...**
	brauy maug **te**-le-f**au**-nah ye...
Mr Brun, please	**Gospodina Bruna, molim**
	gaus-poh-dee-na **bru**-na, **mau**-leem
extension...	**lokal broj...**
	lau-kahl brauy...

FACE TO FACE

A Halo
hah-loh
Hello

B Molim vas, mogu li dobiti...
m**au**-leem vas, **mau**-goo lee **dau**-bee-tee...
I'd like to speak to..., please

A Tko zove?
tkoh **zau**-ve?
Who's calling?

B Ovdje Angela
auv-dye **an**-je-lah
It's Angela

A Samo trenutak…
sah-moh tre-**noo**-tack…
Just a moment…

Can I speak to…?	Mogu li dobiti…?
	mau-goo lee **dau**-bee-tee…?
I'll call back later	Zvat ću kasnije
	zvaht choo **kahs**-nee-ye
I'll call back tomorrow	Zvat ću sutra
	zvaht choo **soot**-rah
This is Mr…/Mrs…	Ovdje gospodin…/gospođa…
	auv-dye gaus-**pau**-deen…/
	gaus-pau-jah…
How do I get an outside line?	Kako mogu dobiti vanjsku liniju?
	kah-koh **mau**-goo **dau**-bee-tee
	vahny-skoo **lee**-nee-yoo?

YOU MAY HEAR…

Pokušavam vas spojiti	I'm trying to connect you
pau-koo-sha-vam vahs	
spau-yee-tee	
Linija je zauzeta, molim pokušajte kasnije	The line is engaged, please try later
lee-nee-yah ye **zah**-oo-ze-tah,	
mau-leem **pau**-koo-sha-yte	
kahs-nee-ye	

Telephone and mobile

81

Želite li ostaviti poruku? **zhe**-lee-te lee **aus**-tah-vee-tee **pau**-roo-koo?	Do you want to leave a message?
...Nakon zvučnog signala ostavite poruku ...**nah**-kon **zvooch**-naug see-**gna**-lah **aus**-tah-vee-te **pau**-roo-koo	...leave a message after the tone
Molim isključite sve mobilne telefone **mau**-leem **ees**-kly-oo-chee-te sve **mau**-beel-ne te-le-**phau**-ne	Please switch off all mobile phones

Text messaging

SMS is very much in use in Croatia.

I will text you	**Poslat ću vam sms poruku** **pau**-slaht choo vahm **es-em-es** **pau**-roo-koo
Can you text me?	**Možete li mi poslati sms?** **mau**-zhe-te lee mee nah-**pee**-sah-tee **es-em-es**?

E-mail

•••••••••••••••••••••••••••••••••••••••

An informal way of addressing an e-mail is **Bok** and ending it with **Čujemo se uskoro** (speak to you soon). For more formal e-mails, begin either **Poštovani**... (for a man) and **Poštovana**... (for a woman).

New Message	**Nova poruka**
To	**Za**
From	**Od**
Subject	**Naslov**
cc	**Kopija**
bcc	**Kopija**
Attachment	**Prilog**
Send	**Pošalji**

Do you have an e-mail?	**Imate li e-mail adresu?**
	ee-mah-te lee **ee**-meyl add-re-soo?
What is your e-mail address?	**Koja je vaša e-mail adresa?**
	kau-ya ye **vah**-sha **ee**-meyl add-re-sah?
How do you spell it?	**Kako se to piše?**
	kah-koh se toh **pee**-she?
All one word	**Sve jednom riječju**
	sve **yed**-naum ree-**ye**-chyoo

All lower case	Sve malim slovima
	sve **mah**-leem **slau**-vee-mah
My e-mail address is...	Moja e-mail adresa je...
	moy-ah **ee**-meyl add-**re**-sah ye...
clare.smith @bit.co.uk	clare točka smith at bit točka ko točka uk
	clare **toh**-chkah smith at bit **toh**-chkah koh **toh**-chkah oo-k
Can I send an e-mail?	Mogu li vam poslati e-mail poruku?
	mau-goo lee vahm **paus**-lah-tee **ee**-meyl **pau**-roo-koo?
Did you get my e-mail?	Jeste li dobili moju poruku?
	ye-ste lee **dau**-bee-lee **mau**-yoo **pau**-roo-koo?

Internet

• •

Most computer terminology tends to be in English and you find the same with the internet.

Are there any internet cafés here?	Ima li ovdje internet kafea?
	ee-mah lee **ov**-dyeh **een**-ter-net **kahf**-eh-ah?
How much is it to log on for an hour?	Koliko košta jedan sat?
	kau-lee-koh **kau**-shtah **ye**-dahn saht?

Fax

• •

The code to send faxes to Croatia is **oo 385** plus the Croatian area code without the first 0, e.g. Split 021, Dubrovnik 020, etc.

Addressing a fax

za	to
od	from
datum	date
naslov:	re:
prilog	please find attached
kopija od…	a copy of…
… stranica ukupno	… pages in total

Do you have a fax?	**Imate li fax?** **ee**-mah-te lee phahks?
I want to send a fax	**Želim poslati fax** z**he**-leem **paus**-lah-tee phahks
What is your fax number?	**Koji je vaš broj faxa?** **kau**-yee ye vahsh brauy **phah**-ksah?
My fax number is…	**Moj broj faxa je**… moy brauy **phah**-ksah ye…

Practicalities

Money

Banks are open from approx. 8.30 am to 1.30 pm
Mon. to Fri. (and sometimes also from 3 to 4 pm).
The kuna is the currency of Croatia. Euros can be
used or changed at exchange bureaux mjenjačnica
mye-nyach-**nee**-tsah or banks banka **bahn**-kah.

kreditna kartica **kre**-deet-nah **kahr**-tee-tsah	credit card
bankomat **bahn**-koh-maht	cash dispenser
blagajna **blah**-gahy-nah	cashiers

Where can I change some money?	Gdje mogu promijeniti nešto novaca? gdye **mau**-goo **prau**-mee-ye-nee-tee **nesh**-toh **nauv**-tsa?
When does the bank open?	Kada se banka otvara? kahda se **bahn**-kah **aut**-va-rah?

When does the bank close?	Kad se banka zatvara?
	kahd se **bahn**-kah **zaht**-va-rah?
Can I pay with...?	Mogu li platiti...?
	mau-goo lee **plah**-tee-tee...?
euros	eurima
	e-**oo**-ree-mah
Swiss francs	švicarskim francima
	shvee-**tsar**-skeem **phrahn**-tsee-mah
I want to change these traveller's cheques	Želim promijeniti ove putničke čekove
	zhe-leem **prau**-mee-ye-**nee**-tee **au**-ve **poot**-neech-ke **check**-au-ve
Where is the nearest cash dispenser?	Gdje je najbliži bankomat?
	gdye ye **nahy**-blee-zhee **bahn**-koh-maht?
Can I use my credit card at the cash dispenser?	Mogu li koristiti kreditnu karticu na bankomatu?
	mau-goo lee **koh**-rees-tee-tee **kre**-deet-noo **kahr**-tee-tsoo nah **bahn**-koh-mah-too?
Do you have any loose change?	Oprostite, imate li sitniša?
	aup-raus-tee-te, **ee**-mah-te lee **seet**-neeshah?

Paying

•••••••••••••••••••••••••••••••••••••••

In Croatia it is illegal to leave a shop, bar, etc.,
without a receipt.

How much is it?	**Koliko to košta?** **kau**-lee-koh toh **kaush**-tah?
How much will it be?	**Koliko će to koštati?** **kau**-lee-koh che toh **kaush**-tah-tee?
Can I pay by...?	**Mogu li platiti...?** **mau**-goo lee **plah**-tee-tee...?
credit card	**kreditnom karticom** **kre**-deet-naum **kahr**-tee-tsaum
cheque	**čekom** **check**-aum
Is service included?	**Da li je uračunata usluga?** da lee ye **oo**-rah-**choo**-nah-ta **oo**-sloo-gah?
Is tax included?	**Je li uračunat porez?** ye lee **pau**-rez **oo**-rah-**choo**-naht?
Put it on my bill	**Stavite to na moj račun** **sta**-vee-te toh nah moy **rah**-choon
Where do I pay?	**Gdje mogu platiti?** gdye m**au**-goo **plah**-tee-tee?
I need a receipt, please	**Trebam račun, molim vas** t**re**-bahm **rah**-choon, **mau**-leem vas

Do I pay in advance?	**Trebam li platiti unaprijed?**
	tre-bahm lee **plah**-tee-tee oo-**nah**-pree-yed?
Do I need to pay a deposit?	**Trebam li ostaviti polog?**
	tre-bahm lee o-s**ta**-vee-tee **pau**-log?
I'm sorry	**Žao mi je**
	zhah-oh mee ye
I've nothing smaller (no change)	**Nemam manju novčanicu/ nemam sitnoga**
	ne-mahm **mah**-nyoo **nauv**-chah-nee-tsoo/**ne**-mahm **seet**-nau-gah

PDV je uračunat peh-deh-veh ye **oo**-rah-**choo**-naht	VAT is included
Usluga je uračunata, ali ne i napojnica **oo**-sloo-gah ye **oo**-rah-**choo**-nah-ta, **ah**-lee ne ee **nah**-poy-nee-tsah	Service is included but not a tip
Platite na blagajni **plah**-tee-te nah **blah**-gahy-nee	Pay at the till
Prvo uzmite račun/ potvrdu na blagajni prvau **oo**-zmee-te **rach**-oon/ **paut**-vr-doo nah **blah**-gahy-nee	First get a receipt/chit at the till (at airport, station bars, etc.)

Paying

89

Luggage

podizanje prtljage **pau**-dee-zah-nye prt-**lyah**-ge	baggage reclaim
ured za izgubljene stvari oo-red zah **eez**-goob-**lye**-ne **stvah**-ree	"lost luggage"
kolica za prtljagu **kau**-lee-tsah zah prt-**lyah**-goo	luggage trolley

My luggage hasn't arrived	Moja prtljaga nije stigla **mo**y-ah prt-**lyah**-gah **nee**-ye **stee**-glah
My suitcase has been damaged on the flight	Moja putna torba je oštećena za vrijeme leta **mo**y-ah **poot**-nah **taur**-bah ye **aush**-te-che-nah zah **vree**-ye-me **le**-ta

Repairs

This is broken	Ovo je pokvareno **au**-vo ye oo pau-**kvah**-re-noh

> **Train** (p 30) > **Air travel** (p 37)

Practicalities

Where can I have this repaired?	Gdje to mogu dati na popravak?
	gdye to **mau**-goo **dah**-tee nah **paup**-rah-vack?
Is it worth repairing?	Vrijedi li to popraviti?
	vr-ee-**ye**-dee lee toh **paup**-rah-vee-tee?
Can you repair...?	Možete li popraviti...?
	mau-zhe-te lee **paup**-rah-**vee**-tee...?
this	ovo
	au-vo
these shoes	ove cipele
	au-ve **tsee**-pe-le
my watch	moj sat
	moy saht

YOU MAY HEAR...

| Žao mi je, ali mi to ne možemo popraviti | Sorry, but we can't mend it |
| zhow mee ye, **ah**-lee mee toh ne **mau**-zhe-moh **paup**-rah-vee-tee | |

Repairs

> **Breakdown** (p 44)

Laundry

. . . .

kemijska čistionica ke-meey-skah **chees**-tee-**au**-nee-tsah	dry-cleaner's
kemijsko čišćenje **ke**-meey-skoh **cheesh**-che-ny-e	dry-cleaning
prašak za rublje **pr-ah**-shak zah **roob**-lye	soap powder
bjelilo **bye**-lee-loh	bleach
stroj za rublje stroy zah **roob**-ly-e	washing machine

Where can I wash these clothes?	**Gdje mogu oprati ovu odjeću?** **gd**-ye **mau**-goo **aup**-rah-tee **au**-voo **au**-dye-choo?
Where is the nearest launderette?	**Gdje je najbliža praonica odjeće?** **gd**-ye ye **ny-blee**-zhah **prow**-nee-tsah **au**-dye-che?

Complaints

. . . .

This does not work	**Ovo ne radi** **au**-vo ne **rah**-dee

Practicalities

It's dirty	Ovo je prljavo
	au-vo ye **pr**-lya-voh
The ... does not work	... ne radi
	... ne **rah**-dee
The ... do not work	... ne rade
	... ne **rah**-de
light	svjetlo
	svye-tloh
toilet	WC/zahod
	ve-tse/**zah**-haud
heating	grijanje
	gr-ee-**ya**h-ny-e
air conditioning	klimatizacija
	klee-**mah**-tee-**zah**-tsee-yah
It's broken	Pokvareno je
	poh-kva-reno ye
I want a refund	Ja želim povrat novca
	ya **zhe**-lee-m **pauv**-raht **nauv**-tsah

Problems

. . . .

Can you help me?	Možete li mi pomoći?
	mau-zhe-te lee mee **pau**-moh-chee?
I speak very little Croatian	Govorim samo malo hrvatskog
	gau-vau-ree-m **sah**-moh **mah**-loh **hr**-**vaht**-tskog

> **Hotel desk** (p 51)

Does anyone here speak English?	Da li ovdje itko govori engleski?
	dah lee **auv**-dye eet-koh **gau**-vau-ree **eng**-**les**-kee?
What's the matter?	U čemu je problem?
	oo **che**-moo ye **praub**-lem?
I would like to speak to whoever is in charge of...	Želim razgovarati s odgovornim za...
	zhe-leem raz-**gau**-vau-rah-tee s **aud**-gau-**vaur**-neem zah...
I'm lost (fem.)/(masc.)	Ja sam zalutala/zalutao
	ya sahm **zah**-loo-tah-lah/**zah**-loo-tow
How do you get to...	Kako mogu doći do...
	kah-koh **mau**-goo **dau**-chee dau...
I missed my train/ plane/ connection	Pobjegao mi je/vlak/ zrakoplov/prijevoz
	poh-bye-gow/**prau**-poos-teo vlahk/ **zrah**-koh-plauv/**pr**-ee-**ye**-vauz
I've missed my flight because there was a strike (fem.)/(masc.)	Zakasnila/zakasnio sam na let zbog prosvjeda
	zah-kas-nee-lah/**zah**-**kas**-**nee**-**oh** sam nah **le**t zbog **pr**-**aus**-vy-eda
The coach has left without me	Autobus je otišao bez mene
	ow-toh-boos ye **au**-teesh-ow bez **me**-ne
Can you show me how this works, please?	Možete li mi pokazati kako ovo radi, molim vas?
	mau-zhe-te lee mee pau-**kah**-zah-tee **kah**-koh **au**-voh **rah**-dee, **mau**-lee-m vas?

Practicalities

I have lost my money	Izgubila/izgubio sam novce
	e**ez**-goo-bee-lah/**eez**-goo-beo
	sam **nauv**-tse
I need to get to...	Moram stići u...
	mau-rahm **stee**-chee oo...
I need to get in touch with the ... consulate	Moram kontaktirati ... konzulat
	mau-rahm **kaun**-tackt-**eer**a-tee
	... **kaun**-zoo-**lah**t
Leave me alone!	Ostavite me na miru!
	aust-ah-**vee**-te me nah **mee**-roo!
Go away!	Odlazite!
	aud-lah-zee-te!

Emergencies

hitna pomoć **heet**-na **pau**-mauch	ambulance
vojna policija **vauy**-nah **pau**-lee-tsee-yah	military police
policija **pau**-lee-tsee-yah	police
vatrogasci **vaht**-rau-**gahs**-tsee	firemen
vatrogasna brigada **vaht**-rau-**gahs**-nah **bree**-gadah	fire brigade
policijska postaja **pau**-lee-tseey-skah **paus**-tah-yah	police station

95

Help!	**Upomoć!**
	oo-paum-auch!
Fire!	**Požar!**
	pau-zhahr!
Can you help me?	**Možete li mi pomoći?**
	mau-zhe-te lee mee **pau**-mau-chee?
There's been an accident!	**Došlo je do nesrece!**
	dohh-shlo ye doh ne-**sre**-che!
Someone...	**Netko...**
	net-koh...
has been injured	**je ozlijeđen**
	ye **auz**-lee-ye-jen
has been knocked down	**je oboren**
	ye o-**boh**-ren
Please call...	**Molim vas zovite...**
	mau-lee-m vas **zau**-vee-te...
the police	**policiju**
	pau-lee-tsee-yu
an ambulance	**hitnu pomoć**
	heet-noo **pau**-mauch
Where is the police station?	**Gdje je policijska postaja?**
	gd-ye ye pau-**lee**-tseey-skah **paus**-tah-yah?
I want to report a crime	**Želim prijaviti zločin**
	zhe-lee-m pree-**yah**-vee-tee **zloh**-cheen

Practicalities

I've been...	**Ja sam …**
	ya sah-m...
robbed	**opljačkana/opljačkan**
(fem.)/masc.)	o-**plyatch**-kah-nah/o-**plyatch**-kahn
attacked	**napadnuta/napadnut**
(fem.)/masc.)	**nah**-pahd-**noo**-tah/**nah**-pahd-noot
Someone's stolen...	**Netko mi je ukrao…**
	net-koh mee ye **oo**-krow...
my bag	**torbu**
	taur-boo
traveller's cheques	**putničke čekove**
	poot-neech-keh **check**-oveh
My car has been broken into	**Netko mi je provalio u auto**
	net-koh mee ye pro-**va**-leeo u **ow**-toh
My car has been stolen	**Auto mi je ukraden**
	ow-toh mee ye **ook**-rah-**de**n
I've been raped	**Silovana sam**
	see-lau-**vah**-nah sah-m
I want to speak to a policewoman	**Želim razgovarati s policajkom**
	zhe-lee-m raz-**gau**-va-**ra**-tee s pau-**lee**-tsay-koh-m
I need to make a telephone call	**Želim telefonirati**
	zhe-leem **te**-le-**faun**-eera-tee

I need a report for my insurance	Potreban mi je izvještaj za osiguranje
	pau-**tre**-bahn mee ye **eez**-vye-shtay zah **aus**-ee-goo-**rah**-ny-e
I didn't know there was a speed limit (fem.)/masc.)	Ja nisam znala/znao za ograničenje brzine
	ya **nee**-sah-m **znah**-lah/znow zah **aug**-rah-nee-**che**-nye br-**zee**-ne
How much is the fine?	Koliko je kazna?
	kau-lee-koh ye **kah**z-nah?
Where do I pay it?	Gdje mogu platiti?
	gd-ye moh-goo **plah**-tee-tee?
Do I have to pay it straightaway?	Da li moram odmah platiti?
	dah lee **mau**-ram **aud**-mah **plah**-tee-tee?
I'm very sorry, officer	Gospodine policajac, jako mi je žao
	gaus-**pau**-deee-neh **pau**-lee-tsah-yats, **yah**-koh mee ye zhow

Health

Pharmacy

Ljekarna **lye**-kahr-nah	pharmacy/chemist
dežurna ljekarna **de**-zhoor-nah **lye**-kahr-nah	duty chemist

Can you give me something for...?	**Možete li mi dati nešto protiv...?** **mau**-zhee-te lee mee **dah**-tee **nesh**-toh **prau**-teev...?
a headache	**glavobolje** **glah**-vau-**bau**-lye
car sickness	**povraćanja u autu** **pauv**-rah-**chah**-nyah oo **ow**-too
a cough	**kašlja** **kahsh**-lyah
diarrhoea	**proljeva** **proh**-lyeva

Is it safe for children?	**Da li je to sigurno za djecu?**
	dah lee lye toh **see**-goor-noh zah **dye**-tsoo?
How much should I give him?	**Koliko da mu dam?**
	kau-lee-koh da moo dahm?

Tri puta na dan...	Three times a day...
tree **poo**-tah nah dahn...	
prije	before
pr-**ee**-ye	
Uz	with
sah	
nakon ... obroka	after ... meals
nah-kon **aub**-rau-kah	

Body

I've broken my leg (fem./masc.)	**Slomila/slomio sam nogu**
	s**lau**-mee-lah/**slau**-meo sahm **nau**-goo
He's hurt his foot	**On je ozlijedio stopalo**
	aun ye **auz**-lee-**ye**-deo **stau**-pah-loh
She's hurt her foot	**Ona je ozlijedila stopalo**
	au-nah ye **auz**-lee-**ye**-dee-lah **stau**-pah-loh

100

Doctor

Bolnica **baul**-nee-tsah	hospital
Hitna pomoć **heet**-nah **pau**-mauch	casualty
Dom zdravlja daum zd**rahv**-lyah	local health centre

FACE TO FACE

A **Bolesna** (fem.)/**bolestan** (masc.) **sam**
bau-les-nah/**bau-les-tan** sahm
I feel ill

B **Imate li temperaturu?**
eee-mah-te lee **tem**-pe-**rah**-too-roo?
Do you have a temperature?

A **Ne, boli me ovdje...**
ne, baul-ee me auv-dye...
No, I have a pain here...

I need a doctor	**Trebam liječnika** **tre**-bahm **lee**-yech-nee-kah
My son is ill	**Moj sin je bolestan** moy seen ye **bau**-les-tahn
My daughter is ill	**Moja kćer je bolesna** **moy**-ah **kch**-er ye **bau**-les-nah
I'm diabetic	**Imam dijabetes** **ee**-mahm **dee**-ya-be-tes

I'm pregnant	**Ja sam trudna**
	ya sahm **trood**-nah
I'm on the pill	**Ja uzimam kontracepcijske tablete**
	ya **ooz**-ee-mahm kon-tra-tsep-tseey-ske **tahb**-le-te
I'm allergic to penicillin	**Ja sam alergična/ alergičan na penicilin**
	ya sahm **ah**-ler-**geech**-nah/ **ah**-ler-**geech**-ahn nah **pe**-nee-**tsee**-leen
Will he/she have to go to hospital?	**Hoće li on/ona morati u bolnicu?**
	hau-che lee aun/**au**-nah **mau**-rah-tee oo **baul**-nee-tsoo?
When are visiting hours?	**Kad je vrijeme za posjete?**
	kahd ye **vree**-ye-me zah **paus**-ye-te?
Will I have to pay?	**Moram li platiti?**
	mau-ram lee **plah**-tee-tee?
How much will it cost?	**Koliko će to koštati?**
	kau-lee-koh che toh **kaush**-tah-tee?
Can you give me a receipt for the insurance?	**Možete li mi dati potvrdu za osiguranje?**
	mau-zhe-te lee mee **dah**-tee **paut**-vr-doo zah **aus**-ee-goo-**rah**-ny-e?

> **Emergencies** (p 95)

| Morat ćete u bolnicu mau-raht **che**-te oo **baul**-nee-tsoo | You will have to go to hospital |
| To nije ozbiljno toh **nee**-ye **au**-zbily-noh | It's not serious |

Dentist

• •

I need a dentist	**Ja trebam zubara** ya **tre**-bahm **zoo**-bah-rah
He/She has toothache	**On/Ona ima zubobolju** aun/**au**-nah **ee**-mah **zoo**-bau-**bau**-lyoo
Can you do a temporary filling?	**Radite li privremene plombe?** **rah**-dee-te lee **pree**-vre-me-ne **plaum**-be?
It hurts	**To boli** toh **bau**-lee
Can you give me something for the pain?	**Možete li mi dati nešto protiv boli?** **mau**-zhe-te lee mee **dah**-tee **nesh**-toh **prau**-teev **bau**-lee?
Can you repair my dentures?	**Možete li popraviti moju protezu?** **mau**-zhe-te lee **paup**-rah-vee-tee **mau**-yoo **prau**-te-zoo?

Do I have to pay?	**Trebam li platiti?**
	tre-bahm lee **plah**-tee-tee?
How much will it be?	**Koliko će to biti?**
	kau-lee-koh che toh **bee**-tee?
Can I have a receipt for my insurance?	**Mogu li dobiti potvrdu za osiguranje?**
	mau-goo lee **dau**-bee-tee **paut**-vr-doo zah **aus**-ee-goo-**rah**-ny-e?

YOU MAY HEAR...

Morat ću vam izvaditi zub	I'll have to take it out
mau-raht choo vahm **eez**-vah-dee-tee zoob	
Potrebno vam je plombirati zub	You need a filling
poh-**tre**-bnoh vahm je **plaum**-bee-ra-tee-zoob	
Ovo može malo zaboljeti	This might hurt a little
au-voh **mau**-zhe **mah**-loh za-**bau**-lye-tee	

> **Pharmacy** (p 99)

Different types of travellers

Disabled travellers

. . . .

What facilities do you have for disabled people?	**Koja pomagala/olakšice imate za invalide?** **kau**-ya **pau**-mah-**gah**-lah/ **au**-lahk-**shee**-tse ee-mah-te zah **een**-vah-**lee**-de?
Are there any toilets for the disabled?	**Imate li toalet za invalide?** **ee**-mah-te lee toh-ah-**let** zah **een**-vah-**lee**-de?
Do you have any bedrooms on the ground floor?	**Imate li jednu sobu u prizemlju?** **ee**-mah-te lee **ee**-yed-noo **sau**-boo oo **pree**-zem-lyoo?
Is there a lift?	**Imate li dizalo?** ye lee too **dee**-zah-loh?
Where is the lift?	**Gdje je dizalo?** gdye ye **dee**-zah-loh?
Can you visit ... in a wheelchair?	**Da li je moguće ići ... u invalidskim kolicima?** **da** lee ye **mau**-goo-che ee-chee ... oo **een**-vah-**leed**-skeem **kau**-lee-tsee-mah?

Do you have wheelchairs?	**Imate li invalidska kolica?** **ee**-mah-te lee **een**-vah-**leed**-skah **kau**-lee-tsah?
Where is the wheelchair-accessible entrance?	Gdje je pristup za invalidska kolica? **gd**-**ye** ye **prees**-toop zah **een**-vah-**leed**-skah **kau**-lee-tsah?
Do you have an induction loop?	**Imate li priključak za gluhonijeme?** **ee**-mah-te lee **preek**-lyoo-chack zah **gloo**-hau-**nee**-ye-me?
Is there a reduction for disabled people?	**Imate li popust za manje sposobne osobe?** **ee**-mah-te lee **paup**-oost zah **mah**-nye **spau**-saub-ne **aus**-au-be?
Is there somewhere I can sit down?	Oprostite, mogu li sjesti negdje? **au**-**praus**-tee-te, **mau**-goo lee **sy**-es-tee **neg**-dy-e?

With kids

Public transport is free for children under 4.
Children between 4 and 12 pay half price.

> **Hotel** (p 49)

A child's ticket	**Ulaznicu za dijete**	
	oo-lahz-**nee**-tsu zah **dee**-ye-te	
He/She is ... years old	**On/ona ima ... godina**	
	aun/**au**-nah **ee**-mah ... **gau**-dee-nah	
Is there a reduction for children?	**Imate li popust za djecu?**	
	ee-mah-te lee **paup**-oost zah **dy**-e-tsoo?	
Do you have a children's menu?	**Imate li jelovnik za djecu?**	
	ee-mah-te lee **y**-**e**-lauv-neek zah **dy**-**e**-tsoo?	
Is it OK to take children?	**Je li u redu povesti djecu?**	
	ye lee oo **re**-doo **pau**-ves-tee **dye**-tsoo?	
Do you have...?	**Imate li...?**	
	ee-mah-te lee...?	
a high chair	**visoku stolicu**	
	vee-sau-koo **stau**-lee-tsoo	
a cot	**kolijevku**	
	koh-lee-yev-koo	
I have two children	**Ja imam dvoje djece**	
	ya **ee**-mah **dvau**-ye dye-tse	
He/She is 8 years old	**On/ona ima osam godina**	
	aun/**au**-nah **ee**-mah **aus**-ahm **gau**-dee-nah	
Do you have any children?	**Imate li djece?**	
	ee-mah-te lee **dye**-tse?	

With kids

> **Pharmacy** (p 99) > **Doctor** (p 101)

Reference

Alphabet

Q, W, X and Y are not native to the Croatian language. You will only see these letters in foreign words. Below are the words used for clarification when spelling something out.

Kako se to piše? **kah**-ko se toh **pee**-she?	How do you spell it?
A kao Ana, B kao Bok a kow ah-nah, b kow bauk	A like Ana, B like Bok

A	a	Ana	**ah**-nah
B	b	Bok	b**auk**
C	c	Cres	tsr-es
Č	č	Čempres	tch-**em**-pres
Ć	ć	Ćevapčić	che-**vap**-tcheech
D	d	Dubrovnik	**doo**-br-auv-neek
DŽ	dž	Džemper	j**em**-per
Đ	đ	Đerdan	**jer**-dahn
E	e	Eko	**e**-koh
F	f	Frula	fr-**oo**-lah

G	g	Grad	gr-**ahd**
H	h	Hvar	hv-**a**hr
I	i	Istra	**ee**s-trah
J	j	Jadran	**yad**-rahn
K	k	Korčula	**kaur**-choo-lah
L	l	Lastovo	**lah**-stau-voh
LJ	lj	Ljepota	**lye**-poh-tah
M	m	Makarska	**mah**-kahr-skah
N	n	Novalja	**nauv**-ah-lyah
O	o	Opatija	**aup**-ah-tee-ya
P	p	Pula	**poo**-lah
R	r	Rijeka	**ree**-ye-kah
S	s	Split	spleet
Š	š	Šibenik	**shee**-be-neek
T	t	Trogir	tr**au**-geer
U	u	Uvala	**oo**-vah-la
V	v	Vis	vees
Z	z	Zadar	**zah**-dah-r
Ž	ž	Život	**zhee**-vaut

Measurements and quantities

• •

1 lb = approx. 0.5 kilo   1 pint = approx. 0.5 litre

Liquids

1/2 litre of...	**pola litre...**
	pau-lah **leet**-reh...
a litre of...	**litru...**
	lee-trooh...
1/2 bottle of...	**pola boce...**
	pau-lah bau-tse...
a bottle of...	**bocu...**
	bau-tsooh...
a glass of...	**čašu...**
	cha-shooh...

Weights

100 grams	**100 grama**
	stoh **grah**-mah
1/2 kilo of...	**pola kile...**
	pau-lah **kee**-leh...
a kilo of...	**kilu...**
	kee-looh...

Food

a slice of...	**krišku...**
	kreesh-kooh...
a portion of...	**porciju...**
	paur-tsee-yoo...

a dozen...	tucet...
	too-tset...
a box of...	kutiju...
	koo-tee-yoo...
a packet of...	paket...
	pa-cket...
a tin of...	limenku...
	lee-men-kooh...
a can of...(beer)	limenku ... (piva)
	lee-men-kooh pee-vah...
a jar of...	teglicu...
	teg-lee-tsooh...

Miscellaneous

...euro worth of...	za ... eura...
	zah ... **e-oor**-ah ...
a quarter	četvrt
	tche-tvrt
20 per cent	dvadeset posto
	dvah-de-set **paus**-toh
more than...	više od...
	vee-she aud...
less than...	manje od...
	mah-nye aud...
double	duplo
	doop-lau
twice	dvaput
	dvah-poot

Numbers

0	**ništica**	**neesh**-tee-tsa
1	**jedan**	**ye**-dahn
2	**dva**	dvah
3	**tri**	tree
4	**četiri**	**che**-tee-ree
5	**pet**	pet
6	**šest**	shest
7	**sedam**	**se**-dahm
8	**osam**	**aus**-ahm
9	**devet**	**dev**-et
10	**deset**	**des**-et
11	**jedanaest**	**y-e**-dahn-ah-est
12	**dvanaest**	**dvah**-nah-est
13	**trinaest**	**tree**-nah-est
14	**četrnaest**	**chet**-r-nah-est
15	**petnaest**	**pet**-nah-est
16	**šesnaest**	**shes**-nah-est
17	**sedamnaest**	se-**dahm**-nah-est
18	**osamnaest**	aus-**ahm**-nah-est
19	**devetnaest**	de-**vet**-nah-est
20	**dvadeset**	**dvah**-de-set
21	**dvadeset jedan**	**dva**-de-set **ye**-dahn
22	**dvadeset dva**	**dvah**-de-set dvah
23	**dvadeset tri**	**dvah**-de-set tree
24	**dvadeset četiri**	**dvah**-de-set **che**-tee-ree

25	dvadeset pet	**dvah**-de-set pet
26	dvadeset šest	**dvah**-de-set shest
27	dvadeset sedam	**dvah**-de-set **se**-dahm
28	dvadeset osam	**dvah**-de-set **aus**-ahm
29	dvadeset devet	**dvah**-de-set de-vet
30	trideset	**tree**-de-set
40	četrdeset	**che-tr**-de-set
50	pedeset	**pe**-de-set
60	šezdeset	**shez**-de-set
70	sedamdeset	se-**dahm**-de-set
80	osamdeset	aus-**ahm**-de-set
90	devedeset	**de**-ve-de-set
100	sto	stoh
110	sto deset	stoh **de**-set
1000	tisuća	**tee**-soo-chah
2000	dvije tisuće	**dvee**-y-e **tee**-soo-che
million	milijun	**mee**-lee-yoon
billion	milijarda	**mee**-lee-**yar**-dah

1st	**první** pr-vee	6th	**šesti** **she**-stee
2nd	**drugi** dr-**oo**-gee	7th	**sedmi** **sed**-mee
3rd	**treći** **tre**-chee	8th	**osmi** **aus**-mee
4th	**četvrti** **che**-tv-r-tee	9th	**deveti** **de**-ve-tee
5th	**peti** **pe**-tee	10th	**deseti** **de**-se-tee

Days and months

Days

Monday	**ponedjeljak**	pau-**ne**-dye-lyack
Tuesday	**utorak**	**oo**-tau-rack
Wednesday	**srijeda**	sree-**ye**-dah
Thursday	**četvrtak**	che-**tvr**-tack
Friday	**petak**	**pe**-tack
Saturday	**subota**	**soo**-bau-tah
Sunday	**nedjelja**	**ne**-dy-e-lyah

Months

January	**siječanj**	see-**ye**-chahny
February	**veljača**	**ve**-lya-chah
March	**ožujak**	**auzh**-oo-yack
April	**travanj**	**trah**-vah-ny
May	**svibanj**	**svee**-bahny
June	**lipanj**	**lee**-pahny
July	**srpanj**	sr-**pahny**
August	**kolovoz**	**kau**-lau-vauz
September	**rujan**	**roo**-yahn
October	**listopad**	**lee**-stau-pahd
November	**studeni**	**stoo**-de-nee
December	**prosinac**	**prau**-see-nats

Seasons

spring	**proljeće**	**prau**-lye-che
summer	**ljeto**	**lye**-toh
autumn	**jesen**	**ye**-sen
winter	**zima**	**zee**-mah

What is today's date?	**Koji je danas datum?**
	kau-yee ye **dah**-nahs **dah**-toom?
What day is it today?	**Koji je danas dan?**
	kau-yee ye **dah**-nahs dahn?

It's the 5th of March 2007	**Danas je peti ožujak dvije tisuće i sedme** **dah**-nahs ye **pe**-tee **au**-zhoo-yack **dvee**-ye **tee**-soo-che ee **sed**-me
on Saturday	**u subotu** oo **soo**-bau-too
on Saturdays	**subotom** **soo**-bau-tohm
every Saturday	**svake subote** **svah**-ke **soo**-bau-te
this Saturday	**ove subote** **au**-ve **soo**-bau-te
next Saturday	**iduće subote** **ee**-doo-che **soo**-bau-te
last Saturday	**prošle subote** **praush**-le **soo**-bau-te
in June	**u lipnju** oo **leep**-nyoo
at the beginning of June	**početkom lipnja** **pau**-chet-kom **leep**-nya
at the end of June	**krajem lipnja** **kra**-yem **leep**-nya
before summer	**prije ljeta** **pree**-ye **lye**-tah
during the summer	**tijekom ljeta** **tee**-ye-kaum **lye**-tah
after summer	**nakon ljeta** **nah**-kaun **lye**-tah

Time

• •

The 24-hour clock is used a lot more in Croatia
than in Britain. After 1200 midday, it continues:
1300 **tree**-nah-est **trinaest**; 1400 **che-tr**-nah-est
četrnaest; 1500 **pet**-nah-est **petnaest**, etc. until
2400 **dvah**-de-set **che**-tee-ree **dvadeset četiri**.
Both the 24 and the 12 hour clock are used in
colloquial Croatian.

What time is it, please?	**Molim vas, koliko je sati?**
	mau-lee-m vas, **kau**-lee-koh ye **sah**-tee?
It's...	**Sad je...**
	sahd ye...
2 o'clock	**dva sata**
	dvah **sah**-tah
3 o'clock	**tri sata**
	tree **sah**-tah
6 o'clock (etc.)	**šest sati**
	shest **sah**-tee
It's 1 o'clock	**Sad je jedan sat**
	sahd ye **ye**-dahn saht
It's midday	**Podne je**
	paud-ne ye
It's midnight	**Ponoć je**
	p**au**-nauch ye

9	devet
	de-vet **sah**-tee
9.10	devet i deset
	de-vet **sah**-tee ee **de**-set
quarter past 9	devet i četvrt
	de-vet ee **che**-tv-rt *or*
	devet i petnaest
	de-vet ee **pet**-nah-est
9.20	devet i dvadeset
	de-vet ee **dvah**-de-set
half past 9	pola deset
	paul-ah **de**-set *or*
	devet i pol
	de-vet ee paul
9.35	dvadeset pet do deset
	dvah-de-set pet dau **de**-set
quarter to 10	petnaest do deset
	pet-nah-est dau **de**-set *or*
	četvrt do deset
	che-tv-rt dau **de**-set
5 minutes to 10	pet minuta do deset
	pet mee-**noo**-tah dau **de**-set

Time phrases

●●●

When does it open/close?	**Kad se otvara/zatvara?** kahd se **aut**-vau-rah/**zaht**-vau-rah?
When does it begin/finish?	**Kad to počinje/završava?** kahd toh **pau**-chee-nye/ **zah**-vr-shah-vah?
at 3 o'clock	**u tri sata** oo tree sah-tah
before 3 o'clock	**prije tri sata** **pree**-ye- tree sah-tah
after 3 o'clock	**nakon tri sata** **nah**-kaun tree sah-tah
today	**danas** **dah**-nahs
tonight	**večeras** ve-**che**-rahs
tomorrow	**sutra** **soo**-trah
yesterday	**jučer** **yoo**-cher

Eating out

Eating places

Bar Many bars serve food: generally salads, sandwiches, pasta dishes and pizzas.

Picerija Pizzas. Eat in or takeaway. Many use wood burning ovens.

Slastičarnica Cake shop. These usually have a café attached where you can sample the cakes, and you can buy ice-cream to go.

Kavana Generally very old-fashioned establishments, a grander type of café, a throwback to the Austro-Hungarian times. They usually offer cakes, coffee, some alcohol and some food.

Gostionica The oldest version of restaurant in Croatia. Usually selling unfussy, sturdy peasant fare. Often very good regional dishes.

Restoran The menu and prices are usually displayed outside the entrance. Restaurants are open from about midday to 2.30 pm and from 7 pm to 10.30 pm.

Sendvič bar Toasted and other sandwiches with extra fillings such as mayonnaise, tomato or gherkin.

Restoran za samoposluživanje Self-service type restaurant which is good for a quick meal.

Cafe bar If you just ask for **crna kava** you'll be served **black coffee**, a tiny strong black coffee, so specify the type of coffee you want.

espreso es-**pre**-sau	strong small black coffee
espresso sa šlagom es-**pre**-sau sah shlah gohm	espresso with whipped cream
cappuccino kah-poo-**chee**-noh	frothy white coffee
instant kava een-**stah**-nt **kah**-vah	instant coffee
bijela kava **bee**-y-e-lah **kah**-vah	coffee with milk
ledeni čaj le-de-mee tchay	iced tea

Eating places

A Što biste naručili?
shtoh **bee**-ste nah-**roo**-chee-lee?
What would you like?

B Čaj s mlijekom, molim
chay s **mlee**-ye-kaum, **mau**-lee-m
A tea with milk, please

a coffee	**kava**	
	kah-vah	
a lager	**pivo**	
	pee-voh	
an orangeade	**narančada**	
	nah-rahn-**cha**-dah	
with lemon	**s limunom**	
	s **lee**-moo-naum	
no sugar	**bez šećera**	
	bez **she**-che-rah	
for two	**za dvoje**	
	zah **dvau**-ye	
for me	**za mene**	
	zah me-ne	
for him/her	**za njega/nju**	
	zah **nye**-gah/nyoo	
for us	**za nas**	
	zah nahs	
with ice	**s ledom**	
	s **le**-daum	

a bottle of	**bocu mineralne vode**
mineral water	**bau**-tsoo **mee**-ne-**rahl**-ne **vau**-de
sparkling	**gaziranu**
	ga-**zee**-rah-noo
still	**negaziranu**
	ne-**ga**-**zee**-rah-noo

Other drinks to try

mirinda non-alcoholic, slightly bitter drink
orangina fizzy soft drink with taste of bitter orange
topla čokolada hot chocolate
pipi orange slightly bitter, non-alcoholic
limunada lemonade
gusti sok thick fruit juice
sok od grejpa grapefruit juice
fanta non-alcoholic fizzy drink

Reading the menu

If you were planning to eat a full Croatian meal, you would begin with **predjelo** (starter), then **glavmo jelo: prvo jelo** (often **juha:** soup) then **drugo jelo** (**meso:** meat: or **riba:** fish), and end with **voće:** fruit or **slatko:** dessert or **kolač:** cake. This requires some time, so people often skip one or two of the courses.

Jelovnik Menu

Predjelo Starter
Juha Soup
Glavno jelo Main course
Voće ili slastice Fruit or cakes

kruh uračunat Tourist menu often includes bread:
samo ručak Set-price menu (lunch only)

In a restaurant

FACE TO FACE

A Ja bih rezervirala (fem.)/rezervirao (masc.)
   za ... osobe
ya beeh **re**-zer-**vee**-rah-la/**re**-zer-**vee**-row
   zah ... **aus**-aub-e
I'd like to book a table for ... people

B Da, za kad?
dah, zah khad?
Yes, when for?

A za večeras.../za sutra uveče.../u osam sati
zah ve-**che**-rahs.../zah **soot**-rah **oo**-ve-cher.../
   oo **aus**-ahm **sah**-tee
for tonight.../for tomorrow night.../at 8 o'clock

Eating out

The menu, please	**Jelovnik, molim**
	ye-lauv-neek, **mau**-lee-m
What is the dish of the day?	**Što je jelo dana?**
	shtoh ye **ye**-lau **dah**-nah?
Do you have a tourist menu?	**Imate li turistički jelovnik?**
	ee-mah-tee lee **too**-rees-**tee**-chkee **ye**-lauv-neek?
at a set price?	**sa cjenikom?**
	sah **tsye**-nee-kaum?
What is the speciality of the house?	**Što je specijalitet kuće?**
	shtoh ye **spets**-ee-ya-**lee**-tet **koo**-che?
Can you tell me what this is?	**Možete li mi kazati što je ovo?**
	mau-zhe-te lee mee **kah**-zah-tee shtoh ye **auv**-oh?
I'll have this	**Ja bih ovo**
	ya beeh **auv**-oh
Could we have some more bread/more water, please?	**Možemo li dobiti još kruha/ još vode, molim?**
	mau-zhe-moh lee **daub**-ee-tee yaush **kroo**-hah/yaush **vau**-de, **mau**-lee-m?
The bill, please	**Račun, molim**
	rah-choon, **mau**-lee-m
Is service included?	**Je li usluga uračunata?**
	ye lee **oos**-loo-gah **oo**-rah-**choo**-nah-tah?

Vegetarian

• •

Croatians love good meat but there are more and
more restaurants offering excellent vegetarian
dishes, even vegetarian and vegan restaurants.

Are there any vegetarian restaurants here?	**Ima li ovdje restorana za vegeterijance?** **ee**-mah lee auv-dye res-**toh**-rahna zah **ve**-ge-tah-**ree**-yahn-tse?
Do you have any vegetarian dishes?	**Imate li vegeterijanska jela?** **ee**-mah-te lee **ve**-ge-tah-**ree**-yahn-ska yela?
Which dishes have no meat/fish?	**Koja jela su bez mesa/ribe?** **kau**-yee **ye**-lah soo bez **me**-sah/**reeb**-e?
What fish dishes do you have?	**Koja riblja jela imate?** **kau**-ya **reeb**-lya yela **ee**-mah-te?
I'd like pasta as a main course	**Ja bih pastu kao glavno jelo** ya **bee**-h pah-stoo ka-oh **glahv**-noh **ye**-loh
I don't like meat	**Ja ne volim meso** ya ne **vau**-lee-m **me**-soh
What do you recommend?	**Što nam preporučujete?** shtoh nahm **pre**-pau-**roo**-choo-yoo-te?

Is it made with vegetable stock?	Je li to kuhano s temeljcem od povrća?
	ye lee toh **koo-hah-noh** s te-**mely**-tsem aud **pauv**-r-cha?

Possible dishes

blitva s krumpirom chard with potatoes
minestrone minestrone (Italian vegetable soup)
vrganji porcini mushrooms
miješana salata mixed salad (lettuce, tomato, peppers, etc.)
jaja s tartufima eggs with truffles
razne paste various pasta dishes
sir, rajčice i svježi bosiljak mozzarella, tomato and fresh basil
gusta juha od povrća thick vegetable soup
pasta s umakom od rajčica pasta with tomato sauce
špageti pesto spaghetti pesto
pasta povera pasta with garlic, lemon, olive oil, basil
paprika i umak od rajčica peppers in tomato sauce
različite pice od povrća various vegetarian pizzas
kuhana riža s maslacom, češnjakom i crnim paprom boiled rice with butter, garlic, black pepper

Wines and spirits

The wine list, please	**Vinsku listu, molim**
	lees-too **vee**-nah, **mau**-lee-m
white wine	**bijelo vino**
	bee-ye-loh **vee**-noh
red wine	**crno vino**
	tsr-noh **vee**-noh
Can you recommend a good local wine?	**Možete li mi preporučiti dobro lokalno vino?**
	mau-zhe-te lee mee **pre**-pau-**roo**-chee-te **daub**-rau **lo**-kal-noh **vee**-noh?
A bottle...	**Bocu...**
	bau-tsoo...
A carafe...	**vrč...**
	vrtch...
of house wine	**domaćeg vina**
	dau-mah-cheg **vee**-nah

Wines

Vinska lista: wine list:

Bakarska vodica sparkling sweet or semi-sweet white
Dingač light, dry red or rosé wine from the Peljesac peninsula
Babić superior, powerful red wine

Pošip full, fruity white wine from Korcula

Plavac light red wine from the Adriatic

Graševina dry, light and fragrant white wines
   from the continent

Grabovac slightly sparkling wine

Plavina good, dry red wine

Rizling sweet, aromatic white wine

Malvazija crisp, smooth, dry white wine

stolno vino table wine

domaće vino house wine

sortno vino selected wine

Spirits and liqueurs

What liqueurs do you have?	Koje likere imate?
	kau-ye **lee**-ke-re **ee**-mah-te?

Kruškovac strong, sweet pear liqueur

Orahovac strongly flavoured walnut-based digéstif

Travarica slightly bitter, herb-flavoured spirit
   to help digestion

Lozovača strong spirit distilled from grape
   pressings (grappa)

Maraschino made of distilled cherries

Pelinkovac strong herb-flavoured digéstif

Konjak Croatian cognac

Šljivovica strongly flavoured plum-based spirit

Vermut Vermouth

Prošek sweet Croatian dessert wine

Menu reader

ananas pineapple
aperitiv aperitif

bademi almonds
bakalar cod
  bakalar s rajčicama salt cod in tomato sauce
banana banana
bezalkoholna pića non-alcoholic drinks
bijela kava coffee with milk
bijela morska riba (po izboru) sea fish (a selection)
bijelo vino white wine
bistra goveđa juha beef consommé
bosiljak basil
brancin seabass
brudet or brujet Croatian bouillabaisse (fish stew)
bubreg kidney

celer celery
crna kava small, strong, black coffee
crno vino red wine
crveno vino rosé wine
cvjetača cauliflower

čaj (kamilica, šipak, metvica) herbal tea (camomile, rosehip, mint)

čaj s limunom (tea with lemon)

čaj s mlijekom (tea with milk)

češnjak garlic

ćevapi small, longish meatballs, grilled

čokolada chocolate

   čokoladini chocolates

dalmatinski pršut Dalmatian ham

dimljena slanina smoked bacon

dimljeno meso smoked meat

dinja melon

divlja svinja wild boar

doručak breakfast

dvopek melba toast

espresso sa šlagom espresso with whipped cream

fazan pheasant

   fazan s gljivama pheasant with mushrooms

   fazan s vinom pheasant in wine

feferoni chilli peppers

girice whitebait

glavno jelo main course

gljive mushrooms

   gljive s umakom mushrooms in a sauce

gorčica mustard

131

goveđa juha s jajem beef consommé with egg

govedina beef

govedji gulas beef stew

grašak peas

grejpfrut grapefruit

grožđe grapes

grožđica raisins

gulaš spicy stew of beef, pork or fish

hladna predjela cold starters

hladna zakuska (Pršut, sir, salama, francuska salata, jaja, masline) cold plate (Dalmatian cured, cold smoked and air dried ham, cheese, salami, French salad, egg, olives)

hobotnica na salatu octopus salad

  hobotnica s krumpirima octopus baked with potatoes

hrenovke sa senfom Frankfurters with mustard

instant kava instant coffee

jabuka apple

jaja eggs

jagode strawberries

janje lamb

janjetina suckling or milk-fed lamb, usually eaten at Easter, roasted with garlic and rosemary.

jaretina baby goat (kid)

jastog lobster

jegulja eel

jela na žaru grilled dishes

jela po narudžbi à la carte dishes
jelo dana dish of the day
  jelovnik menu
jetra liver
  jetra na maslacu i luku liver fried in butter and onion
jogurt yoghurt
juha soup
  juha od gljiva mushroom soup
  juha od povrća vegetable soup
  juha od tripica sa sirom rich tripe and cheese soup
  juha riblja seafood soup

kamilica camomile tea
kapućino cappucino
karamele toffee sweets
kava espresso espresso coffee
kisele salate salads of pickled vegetables
kiseli krastavci pickled gherkins
kobasice sausages
kockice leda ice cubes
kolači cakes
komad bubrežnjaka piece of loin
kokos coconut
kokoš hen
koktel cocktail
kompoti compote
kotlet cutlet/chop
krastavac cucumber
krem juhe (rajčica, gljiva ili šparoga) cream soups
  (tomato, mushroom, asparagus)

kroketi od krumpira potato croquettes

kruh bread

krumpiri potatoes

kruške pears

kuhana kobasica boiled sausage

kuhana slanina boiled bacon

kuhani krumpir boiled potatoes

kuhano boiled

kuhano meso i povrće different kinds of meat and
vegetables boiled together

kunić rabbit

kunić u umaku rabbit stew

kupine blackberries

kupus cabbage

kupus salata cabbage salad

leća lentils

ledeni čaj iced tea

lignja squid

lignje na žaru grilled squid

liker liqueur

limenka piva canned beer

limun lemon

lješnjaci hazelnuts

ljuta papričica hot chilli pepper

lokalno jelo local dish

lovorov list bayleaf

lubenica watermelon

luk onion

mahune na maslacu buttered green beans

majoneza mayonnaise

makaroni penne

maline raspberries

mandarine mandarins

marelica apricot

margarin margarine

maruni/kesteni chestnuts

maslac butter

masline olives

maslinovo ulje olive oil

med honey

mesna pašteta pâté

mesna salata meat salad

meso meat

miješana salata (rajčica, krastavac, rotkvica, paprika)
mixed salad, tomatoes, cucumbers, radish, pepper)

mineralna voda mineral water

mješana riba mixed fish

mlijeko milk

mljeveno meso minced meat

morski jež sea urchin

morski plodovi s roštilja selection of grilled seafood

morski račići prawns

morski rak crab

mozak brains, usually fried with eggs

mrkva na maslacu buttered carrots

mrkve carrots

namazi spreads
nar pomegranate
naranče oranges
nektarine nectarines

ocat vinegar
odrezak steak
  odrezak divlje svinje wild boar steaks
  odrezak na žaru grilled steak
omlet omelette
orasi walnuts
osvježavajuće piće refreshing drink
ovčji sir ewe's milk cheese

palačinke (s čokoladom, džemom, orasima) pancakes
  (with chocolate, jam, walnuts)
papar pepper
patka duck
patlidžan aubergine
pečena guska roast goose
pečena patka roast duck
pečena piletina roast chicken
pečena purica roast turkey
pečenica dried cured fillet of pork
pečeno janje roast lamb
pečeno odojče roast suckling pig
pica pizza
  pica od gljiva mushroom pizza
  pica s morskim plodovima pizza with seafood

pica s četiri sira pizza with four cheeses

pica s rajčicama i češnjakom tomato and garlic pizza

pica s rajčicama, inćunima, maslinama pizza with tomato, anchovy, black olives

pica sa rajčicama, češnjakom i ruzmarinom pizza with tomatoes, garlic and rosemary

pica sa šunkom, artičokom i jajima pizza with baby artichoke, ham and egg

pileća prsa chicken breast

pileće jetrice chicken livers

piletina chicken

  piletina na američki način chicken American style

  piletina na žaru grilled chicken

  piletina sa rajčicama i paprikama chicken with tomatoes and peppers

pirjani teleći medaljoni s gljivama veal medallions with mushrooms

pjenušavo bijelo suho vino sparkling dry white wine

pjenušavo vino sparkling wine

pljeskavica burger

  pljeskavica sa sirom ground burger with cheese

pohani sir s tartar umakom deep fried cheese with tartar sauce

pomfrit french fries

predjelo starter/appetizer

prirodni sokovi (naranča, limun) natural fruit juices (orange, lemon)

prošek dessert wine

pršut i dinja Dalmatian ham and melon
pršut s jajima Dalmatian ham with eggs
pržena riba fried fish
pržene lignje deep fried squid rings
prženi krumpir fried potatoes
prženo fried
punjeno stuffed
  punjene lignje stuffed squid
  punjene marelice stuffed apricots
  punjene paprike stuffed peppers
  punjene rajčice stuffed tomatoes
  punjeni luk stuffed onions
  punjeni patlidžani stuffed aubergines
puretina turkey
purica s mlincima a Croatian dish, roast turkey with pasta
puževi snails

rajčica tomato
rajčica, umak od tomato sauce
razna mesa na žaru a choice of grilled meat
razna rižota various types of risotto
riba fish
riblja juha fish soup
riblja plata fish platter
rizi bizi rice with peas, with or without bacon or chicken
riža rice
rižoto (crni) od liganja squid risotto (black with squid ink)
rižoto od gljiva mushroom risotto

rižoto od morskih plodova seafood risotto

rižoto proljetni risotto primavera (spring)

rižoto zlatni risotto with saffron, parmesan and butter

roščić croissant

roštilj spit roast or grilled meat

ručak lunch

ružmarin rosemary

salama salami

salata salad

  salata od govedine beef salad

  salata od hobotnice octopus salad

  salata od morskih plodova seafood salad

  salata od rajčica tomato salad

  salata od riže rice salad

  salata tricolore tomato, basil and mozzarella salad

sardine sardines

  sardine pržene, u octu i luku fried sardines marinated
in vinegar and onions

sardine u ulju, punjene i pržene sardines marinated
and stuffed then fried

savijače (od sira, jabuka) strudels (cheese or apple)

sendvič od dimljene tune smoked tuna sandwich

sendvič od pršuta Dalmatian ham sandwich

sendvič od sira cheese sandwich

sendvič od šunke ham sandwich

sendvič od zimske salami sandwich

sezonsko povrće seasonal vegetables

sezonsko voće (jabuke, naranče, banane, grožđe, marelice, breskve) seasonal fruit (apples, oranges, bananas, grapes, apricots, peaches)

sir cheese

  Edamer Edam cheese

  kozji sir goat's cheese

  kravlji sir cow's cheese

  lički sir smoked cheese from Lika

  meki kozji sir soft goat's cheese

  mladi kravlji sir cottage cheese

  ovčji sir ewe's milk cheese

  Paški sir Pag island cheese

  Trapist Trappist cheese

  Zdenka sir za mazanje Zdenka spreadable cheese

sir pržen na ulju cheese fried in oil

skuša mackerel

sladoled ice cream

slanina bacon

  slanina kuhana boiled bacon

slanina od divlje svinje, kuhana boiled wild boar bacon

slastice desserts

slatke paprike s rajčicama peppers with tomatoes

slatko dessert

slatko vino sweet wine

smokve figs

soda–voda soda water

sokovi juices

sol salt

sortno vino fine wine

s roštilja grilled

škampi scampi

školjke shellfish

špageti Bolognese spaghetti Bolognese

špageti Carbonara spaghetti Carbonara

špageti Milanese spaghetti Milanese

špageti Napoli spaghetti Napoli

špageti s maslacem spaghetti with butter

špageti s plodovima mora spaghetti with seafood

šparoge asparagus

stolno vino table wine

suhomesnati izbor cold meats (ham, salami, mortadella, etc)

suho vino dry wine

suncokret sunflower

svinjetina pork

svinjska noga knuckle of pork

svinjski kotlet pork chop

šećer sugar

škampi (na žaru or buzara) grilled scampi in garlic, olive
  oil, parsley and wine sauce

školjke, dagnje (buzara) shellfish, mussels (buzara)

šljive plums

špageti spaghetti

šparoge asparagus

špinat spinach

štrukle Croatian dish, pasta stuffed with cheese

šumsko voće forest fruits

teleća jetra na venecijanski veal liver Venetian style (sautéed)

teleća jetra na žaru grilled veal liver

teleći odrezak punjen pršutom i sirom veal steak stuffed with ham and cheese

tonik tonic water

topla čokolada hot chocolate

topli i hladni napitci hot and cold drinks

topla predjela warm starters

topli napitci hot drinks

torta cake / flan / tart

torta od sira cheesecake

trešnje cherries

tuna tuna

ulje oil

umak sauce

u maslinovu ulju in olive oil

usluga uračunata service included

vanilija vanilla

variva vegetable stews

večera dinner

vermut vermouth

vinjak brandy

viski whisky

višnje cherries

voće fruit

voćni sok fruit juice

vrhnje cream or kiselo vrhnje, soured cream

waldorf salata Waldorf salad

zajutrak breakfast
zamrznut frozen
zec hare
  zečetina u vinu hare in wine
zelena salata green salad
zelena salata lettuce
zeleni kupus (green) cabbage
žablji bataci frogs legs
žitne pahuljice cereals

Grammar

Nouns

• •

A noun is a word, such as **grad** (city), **knjiga** (book),
selo (village) or **Marko** (Mark) and **Marija** (Maria),
which is used to refer to a person or thing. In Croatian
there are no definite or indefinite articles, such as
'the', 'a' or 'an'. For example, where in English 'the
city', 'the book' and 'the village' are used, in Croatian
no article is used: **grad**, **knjiga** and **selo**.

Croatian nouns are either masculine (**grad**),
feminine (**knjiga**) or neuter (**selo**). The gender of
regular nouns is shown in the following way:

Masculine nouns end in a consonant in the
nominative case: **grad**, **park** (park), **stol** (table), **kolač**
(cake), etc. These nouns decline in the singular and
in the plural. There are seven noun cases when
declining, but in this phrase book we omit the
vocative case to make it easier to learn and
remember. Here are two examples: **grad** and **kolač**.

	singular	plural	singular	plural
Nominative	grad	grad + ovi	kolač	kolač + i
Genitive	grad + a	grad + ova	kolač + a	kolač + a
Dative	grad + u	grad + ovima	kolač + u	kolač + ima
Accusative	grad	grad + ove	kolač	kolač + e
Locative	grad + u	grad + ovima	kolač + u	kolač + ima
Instrumental	grad + om	grad + ovima	kolač + om	kolač + ima

Although regular masculine nouns have no stem changes, single letter or group letter endings are added to the stem following the pattern of declination.

Regular feminine nouns end in the vowel 'a' in the nominative case: knjiga, sestra (sister), voda (water), plaža (beach), etc. These nouns decline in the singular and in the plural. Here are two examples: sestra and plaža.

	singular	plural	singular	plural
Nominative	sestra	sestr + e	plaže	plaž + e
Genitive	sestr + e	sestar + a	plaž + a	plaž + a
Dative	sestr + i	sestr + ama	plaž + i	plaž + ama
Accusative	sestr + u	sestr + e	plaž + e	plaž + e
Locative	sestr + i	sestr + ama	plaž + i	plaž + ama
Instrumental	sestr + om	sestr + ama	plaž + om	plaž + ama

Regular feminine nouns change the last letter when declining.

Regular neuter nouns end in either 'e' or 'o' in the nominative case: selo, more (sea), pivo (beer), etc. These nouns decline in the singular and in the plural. Here are two examples: selo and more.

	singular	plural	singular	plural
Nominative	selo	sel + a	more	mor + a
Genitive	sel + a	sel + a	mor + a	mor + a
Dative	sel + u	sel + ima	mor + u	mor + ima
Accusative	selo	sel + a	more	mor + a
Locative	sel + u	sel + ima	mor + u	mor + ima
Instrumental	sel + om	sel + ima	mor + om	mor + ima

Regular neuter nouns change the last letter when declining.

Note: To remember the connections between nouns and prepositions, it is easier to memorize the noun endings. Used after prepositions, nouns change their endings in the following pattern:

Genitive

	masculine	neuter	feminine
blizu (near)...	grada, stola...	sela, mora...	vode, kuće (house)...
iz (from)...	parka, broda (ship)...	piva, vozila (vehicle)...	ulice (street), knjige...

The other prepositions that go with the Genitive are: **od** (from), **do** (to), **bez** (without), **ispred** (in front of), **ispod** (under), **uz** (next to), **pokraj** (besides).

Locative

	masculine	neuter	feminine
u (in)/ (about)...	gradu, stolu...	selu, moru...	vodi, kući...
po (along)/ **na** (on)...	parka, kolaču...	jezeru (lake)...	ulici, plaži...

The other prepositions that go with the Locative are: **na** (on), **među** (among).

Instrumental

	masculine	neuter	feminine
sa (with)	čovjekom (man)...	vinom (wine)...	sestrom, majkom (mother)...

147

Note: When using certain nouns in the Instrumental, it is not correct to use the prepositions 'sa' or 's', e.g.:

to travel by bus, train, ship, or plane
putovati autobusom, vlakom, brodom ili zrakoplovom
to write with a pencil, fountain pen
pisati olovkom, naliv-perom

Dative

There are only three prepositions, '**k**'/'**ka**' or '**prema**' (to/towards), that are used with nouns in the Dative. Besides these, nouns in the Dative can be used without a preposition, e.g.:

We go to/towards the city
Mi idemo k/ka/prema gradu
We return the book to the library
Mi vratimo knjigu u knjižnicu

Accusative

The preposition '**u**' is the only preposition which goes with nouns in the Accusative. Besides this, nouns in the Accusative can be used without a preposition, e.g.:

We go to the city
Mi idemo u grad
We go to see the city
Mi idemo vidjeti grad

For most regular masculine nouns, singular and plural endings change as follows:

masc. sing.	masc. plur.	Example: grad (city, town)
a	**ovi**	grad+a → grad+**ovi**
u	**ova**	grad+u → grad+**ova**
om	**ove**	grad+**om** → grad+**ove**
	ovima	grad+**ovima**

For most regular feminine nouns, singular and plural endings change as follows:

fem. sing.	fem. neu.	Example: kuća (house)
e	e	kuć+e → kuć+e
i	a	kuć+i → kuć+a
u	ama	kuć+u → kuć+ama
om		kuć+om

For most regular neuter nouns, singular and plural endings change as follows:

neu. sing.	fem. neu.	Example: vozilo (vehicle)
a	a	vozil+a → vozil+a
u	ima	vozil+u → vozil+ima
om		vozil+om

Adjectives

●●●●●●●●●●●●●●●●●●●●●●●●●●●●●●●●●●●●●●

An adjective is a word such as small, pretty or practical that describes a person or thing, or gives extra information about them. In Croatian adjectives normally come before the noun they describe, e.g. <u>crvena</u> jabuka (the <u>red</u> apple), <u>bijelo</u> vino (the white wine), <u>veliki</u> most (the big bridge).

Croatian adjectives reflect the gender of the noun they describe. Adjectives decline and they agree with the nouns they modify. Adjectives are selected by gender: in the Nominative the masculine ending is –i; the feminine ending is –a; and the neuter ending is –o.

Nominative	The big city is far
	<u>Veliki</u> grad je daleko (masc.)
	The big house is far
	<u>Velika</u> kuća je daleko (fem.)
	The big village is far
	<u>Veliko</u> selo je daleko (neut.)
Genitive	We are far away from the big city:
	Mi smo daleko od <u>velikog</u> grada.
	(masc.)

	We are far away from the big house
	Mi smo daleko od <u>velike</u> kuće
	(fem.)
	We are far away from the big village
	Mi smo daleko od <u>velikog</u> sela
	(neut.)
Dative	We go towards...
	Mi idemo prema <u>velikom</u> gradu
	(masc.)
	...**prema <u>velikoj</u> kući** (fem.)
	...**prema <u>velikom</u> selu** (neut.)
Accusative	We go to...
	Mi idemo u <u>veliki</u> grad (masc.)
	...**u <u>veliku</u> kuću** (fem.)
	...**u <u>veliko</u> selo** (neut.)
Locative	We live...
	Mi živimo u <u>velikom</u> gradu
	(masc.) ...**u <u>velikoj</u> kući** (fem.)
	...**u <u>velikom</u> selu** (neut.)
Instrumental	We are happy with...
	Mi smo sretni sa/s <u>velikim</u>
	gradom (masc.)
	...**<u>velikom</u> kućom** (fem.)
	...**<u>velikim</u> selom** (neut.)

Grammar

151

The plural forms of adjectives also change but we will not focus on them in this short grammar section. Adjectives can sometimes follow the noun they describe, some common exceptions are:

The city is beautiful	**Lijep** grad (masc.)
The house is beautiful	**Lijepa** kuća (fem.)
The village is beautiful	**Lijepo** selo (neut.)

Personal pronouns

There are two forms of personal pronouns (long and short), but we will focus only on the long form in this short grammar section.

singular		plural	
I	**ja**	we	**mi**
you	**ti**	you	**vi**
he	**on** (m)	they	**oni**
she	**ona** (f)	they	**one** (f)
it	**ono** (n)	they	**ona** (n)

The declension of pronouns can be more easily remembered if it is learned together with the pronoun. We suggest the following way for remembering pronoun endings:

Nominative: Pronoun + the present tense of the verb 'to be'

I am: **ja** sam, you are: **ti** si, he is: **on** je,
she is: **ona** je, it is: **ono** je, we are: **mi** smo,
you are: **vi** ste, they are: **oni** su

Genitive: for/near/without/next to/from/...
        za/blizu/bez/pokraj/od/...

me	you	him	her	us	you	them
mene	tebe	njega	nju	nas	vas	njih

Dative: towards prema

me	you	him	her	us	you	them
meni	tebi	njemu	njoj	nama	vama	njima

Locative: on na, about o

me	you	him	her	us	you	them
meni	tebi	njemu	njoj	nama	vama	njima

Instrumental: with sa/s

me	you	him	her	us	you	them
mnom	tobom	njim	njom	nama	vama	njima

Possessive pronouns

singular		plural	
My	moj/moja/moje	Our	naš/naša/naše
Your	tvoj/tvoja/tvoje	Your	vaš/vaša/vaše
His	njegov/njegova/ njegovo	Their	njihov/njihova/ njihovo
Her	njen/njena/njeno		

These words depend on the gender and number of the nouns they modify, and not on the gender of the 'owner'.

Nominative

My hotel is there	<u>Moj</u> hotel je tamo
My bag is here	<u>Moja</u> torba je ovdje
My village is small	<u>Moje</u> selo je malo

	masculine	feminine	neuter
My...	Moj...	Moja...	Moje...
Your...	Tvoj...	Tvoja...	Tvoje...
His...	Njegov...	Njegova...	Njegovo...
Her...	Njen...	Njena...	Njeno...
Our...	Naš...	Naša...	Naše...
Your...	Vaš...	Vaša...	Vaše...
Their...	Njihov...	Njihova...	Njihovo...

Genitive

Near my garden	Blizu <u>mog</u> vrta
Near my house	Blizu <u>moje</u> kuće
Near my village	Blizu <u>mog</u> sela

	masculine	feminine	neuter
... my ...	... mog ...	... moje ...	... mog ...
... your...	... tvog ...	... tvoje ...	... tvog ...
... his ...	... njegovog ...	... njegove ...	... njegovog ...
... her ...	... njenog ...	... njene ...	... njenog ...
... our ...	... našeg ...	... naše ...	... našeg ...
... your...	... vašeg ...	... vaše ...	... vašeg ...
... their ...	... nhihovog ...	... njihove ...	... njihovog ...

Accusative

We enter my hotel	Mi ulazimo u moj hotel
...my house	...u moju kuću
...my village	...u moje selo

	masculine	feminine	neuter
... my ...	... moj ...	... moju ...	... moje ...
... your...	... tvog ...	... tvoju ...	... tvoje ...
... his ...	... njegov ...	... njegovu ...	... njegovo ...
... her ...	... njen ...	... njenu ...	... njeno ...
... our ...	... naš ...	... našu ...	... naše ...
... your...	... vaš ...	... vašu ...	... vaše ...
... their...	... njihov ...	... njihovu ...	... njihovo ...

Grammar

Locative

In my town...	U <u>mom</u> gradu...
In my room...	U <u>mojoj</u> sobi...
In my village...	U <u>mom</u> selu...

	masculine	feminine	neuter
... my ...	... mom ...	... mojoj ...	... mom ...
... your...	... tvom ...	... tvojoj ...	... tvom ...
... his ...	... njegovom...	... njegovoj ...	...njegovom...
... her ...	... njenom ...	... njenoj ...	... njenom ...
... our ...	... našem ...	... našoj ...	... našem ...
... your...	... vašem ...	... vašoj ...	... vašem ...
... their...	... njihovom ...	... njihovoj ...	... njihovom ...

The Dative and the Instrumental are the same as the Locative. In this short grammar section we will not focus on the plural form of possessive adjectives.

Pronouns

• •

A pronoun is a word that you use to refer to someone or something when you do not need to use a noun, often because the person or thing has been mentioned earlier. Examples are 'it', 'she', 'they' and 'myself'.

subject		object	
I	ja	me	mene/meni/mnom
you	ti	you	tebe/tebi/tobom
he	on	him	njega/njemu/njim
she	ona	her	nje/nju/njom
we	mi	us	nas/nama
you	vi	you	vas/vama
they	oni	them	njih/njima

The object pronouns shown above are also used to
mean to me, to us, etc., except:

to you	za tebe
to him	za njega
to her	za nju
to it	za to
to us	za nas
to you (pl.)	za vas
to them	za njih

Object pronouns (long form) go after the verb:

Ja vidim <u>njega</u>	I see him
Ja ću pisati <u>njima</u>	I will write to them

Object pronouns (short form) go before the verb:

Ja <u>ga</u> vidim	I see him
Ja ću <u>im</u> pisati	I will write to them

When used with an infinitive (the verb form given in the dictionary), the pronoun follows and is attached to the infinitive:

| I want to buy it | Ja želim kupiti <u>to</u> |

Subject pronouns (ja, ti, on, ona etc.) are often omitted in Croatian, since the verb ending generally distinguishes the person:

govori<u>m</u>	I speak
govori<u>mo</u>	we speak
govor<u>e</u>	they speak

In Croatian there are two forms for you – ti (singular) and vi (plural). Ti, the familiar form for you, should only be used with people you know well, or children.

Verbs

●●●●●●●●●●●●●●●●●●●●●●●●●●●●●●●●●

A verb is a word such as 'sing', 'walk' or 'cry' which is used with a subject to say what someone or something does or what happens to them. Regular verbs follow the same pattern of endings. Irregular verbs do not follow a regular pattern so you need to learn the different endings.

Infinitive Form

There are two basic endings for verbs in the infinitive form. Here are some common verbs:

ti		ći	
govoriti	to speak	ići	to go
raditi	to work	stići	to arrive
piti	to drink	ući	to enter
čitati	to read	poći	to leave, etc.
slušati	to listen, etc.		

Present tense

There are three main patterns of endings for Croatian verbs – those ending in -am, -em and -im. Three examples of regular verbs are shown, since there are three distinct groups of endings. Subject pronouns are shown in brackets because they are often not used:

	ČITATI	TO READ
(ja)	čitam	I read
(ti)	čitaš	you read
(on/ona)	čita	(s)he reads
(mi)	čitamo	we read
(vi)	čitate	you read
(oni)	čitaju	they read

	GOVORITI	**TO SPEAK**
(ja)	**govorim**	I speak
(ti)	**govoriš**	you speak
(on/ona)	**govori**	(s)he speaks
(mi)	**govorimo**	we speak
(vi)	**govorite**	you speak
(oni)	**govore**	they speak

	PITI	**TO DRINK**
(ja)	**pijem**	I drink
(ti)	**piješ**	you drink
(on/ona)	**pije**	(s)he drinks
(mi)	**pijemo**	we drink
(vi)	**pijete**	you drink
(oni)	**piju**	they drink

	IĆI	**TO GO**
(ja)	**idem**	I go
(ti)	**ideš**	you go
(on/ona)	**ide**	(s)he goes
(mi)	**idemo**	we go
(vi)	**idete**	you go
(oni)	**idu**	they go

Grammar

Past tense

To form the simple past tense combine an auxiliary verb (to be **biti**) with the past participle of the main verb, e.g.

I worked
Ja sam *(auxiliary)* **radio** (m)/**radila** (f) *(past participle)*

In Croatian the basic auxiliary verb is **biti** (to be).

	BITI	TO BE	RADITI	TO WORK
(ja)	**sam**	I am	**radi+o** (m) *or* +**la** (f)	I worked
(ti)	**si**	you are	**radi+o** *or* +**la**	you worked
(on/ ona)	**je**	s(he) is	**radio** (m) **radila**	s(he) worked
(mi)	**smo**	we are	**radi+li**	we worked
(vi)	**ste**	you are	**radili**	you worked
(oni)	**su**	they are	**radili**	they worked

Present tense   Simple past tense

To form the simple past tense, 'I spoke/I have spoken', 'I bought/I have bought', etc. combine the present tense of the verb 'to be' with the past participle of the verb, e.g.

I spoke/	**Ja sam govorio** (masc.)/**govorila**
I have spoken	(fem.) or **govorio/govorila sam**
I bought/	**Ja sam kupio** (masc.)/**kupila**
I have bought	(fem.) or **kupio/kupila sam**

GOVORITI = **TO SPEAK** *(past)*

govorio/govorila sam	I spoke
govorio/govorila si	you spoke
govorio/govorila je	(s)he spoke
govorili smo	we spoke
govorili ste	you spoke
govorili su	they spoke

PROČITATI = **TO READ** *(past)*

pročitao/pročitala sam	I have read
pročitao/pročitala si	you have read
pročitao/pročitala je	(s)he has read
pročitali smo	we have read
pročitali ste	you have read
pročitali su	they have read

POPITI = TO DRINK *(past)*

popio/popila sam	I drank
popio/popila si	you drank
popio/popila je	(s)he drank
popili smo	we drank
popili ste	you drank
popili su	they drank

OTIĆI = TO GO *(past)*

otišao/otišla sam	I went
otišao/otišla si	you went
otišao/otišla je	(s)he went
otišli smo	we went
otišli ste	you went
otišli su	they went

Note: To make a sentence negative e.g. I am not eating, the negative form of 'to be' is placed before the verb.

Ja ne jedem *or* ne jedem *(present)*	I am not eating
Ja nisam išao (m)/išla (f) *or* nisam išla/išao *(past)*	I did not go

To make a sentence negative you have to use the
negative form of the present tense of 'to be' before
the past participle of the verb.

	BITI	TO BE
(ja)	nisam	I am not
(ti)	nisi	you are not
(on/ona)	nije	s(he) is not
(mi)	nismo	we are not
(vi)	niste	you are not
(oni)	nisu	they are not

Irregular verbs

One of the most important irregular verbs is:

	MOĆI	TO BE ABLE		
	(present)		*(past)*	
(ja)	mogu	I can/ I am able	mogao (m)/ mogla sam (f)	I could
(ti)	možeš	you...	mogao/ mogla si	you could...
(on/ona)	može		mogao mogla je	
(mi)	možemo		mogli smo	
(vi)	možete		mogli ste	
(oni)	mogu		mogli ste	

164

Public holidays

On national holidays you may find information offices closed, museums open for shorter hours and public transport running a limited service.

Note that Easter Monday changes every year, while all the other holidays keep to the same date.

January 1	New Year's Day
January 6	Epiphany (Three Kings)
March or April	Easter Day & Easter Monday
May 1	Mayday
June 7	Ascension Day
June 22	Anti-fascist Resistance Day
August 5	Victory Day
August 15	Assumption Day
October 8	Independence Day
November 1	All Saints
December 25	Christmas Day
December 26	St. Stephen's Day (Boxing Day)

English – Croatian

A

able: to be able	moći	mau-chee
about	o	au
above	iznad	eez-nad
abroad	inozemstvo (n)	ee-nau-zems-tvoh
access	pristup (m)	pree-stoop
accident	udes (m)	oo-des
accident & emergency department	Hitna pomoć (f)	heet-nah pau-mauch
accommodation	smještaj (m)	sm-ye-sh-tay
to accompany	pratiti	prah-tee-tee
account (bill)	račun (m)	rah-choon
account (in bank)	bankovni račun	bahn-kauv-nee rah-choon
ache	bol (f)	baul
it aches	to boli	toh bau-lee
address	adresa (f)	add-re-sah
what is the address?	koja je adresa?	kau-ya ye add-re-sah?
admission charge/fee	cijena ulaza	tsee-ye-nah oo-lah-zah
adult	odrastao (m); odrasla (f)	aud-rahs-tow; aud-rahs-lah
advance: in advance	unaprijed	oo-nahpree-y-ed
advice	savjet (m)	sah-vyet
aeroplane	zrakoplov (m) or avion (m)	zrah-kaup-lauv
afraid: to be afraid	biti uplašen (a)(o)	bee-tee oo-plah-shen
after	poslije	paus-lee-ye
afternoon	popodne (n)	pau-paud-ne
again	opet; ponovo	au-pet; pau-nau-voh
against	protiv	prau-teev
age	dob (f)	daub
ago	prije	pree-ye
agreement	pristanak (m)	prees-tah-nahk
air-conditioning	klimatizacija (f)	klee-mah-tee-zah-tsee-ya

English	Croatian	Pronunciation
airplane	avion (m)	ah-ve-on
airport	zračna luka (f)	zrah-tch-nah loo-kah
airline ticket	avionska karta (f)	ah-ve-on-skah kahr-tah
alarm	uzbuna (f)	ooz-boo-nah
alarm clock	budilnik (m)	boo-deel-neek
alcohol	alkohol (m)	ahl-kau-haul
alcohol-free	bezalkoholni (a)(o)	bez-ahl-ko-haul-noh
alcoholic	alkohol(ni)a(o)	ahl-kau-haul-nee
allergic	alergičan(čna)(čno)	ah-ler-gee-chahn
allergy	alergija (f)	ah-ler-gee-ya
to allow	dopustiti	dau-poos-tee-tee
alright (agreed)	u redu	oo re-doo
almost	gotovo	gau-toh-vau
alone	usamljen(a)(o)	oo-sahm-lye-noh
already	već	vech
also	također	tah-koh-jer
always	uvijek	oo-vee-yek
ambulance	bolnička kola (f)	baul-neech-kah kau-lah
America	Amerika (f)	ah-me-ree-kah
American	američki(a)(o)	ah-me-reech-kee
anaesthetic	anestetik (m)	ah-nes-te-teeck
and	i	ee
angry	ljut(a)(o)	lyoot
annual	godišnji(a)(e)	gaud-eesh-nyee
another	još jedan	yaush ye-dahn
answer	odgovor (m)	aud-gauv-aur
antibiotic	antibiotik (m)	ahn-tee-bee-o-teeck
antiseptic	antiseptičan (čna)(čno)	ahn-tee-sep-teech-noh
anyone	itko	eet-koh
anything	išta	ee-shtah
apartment	apartman (m)	ah-pah-rt-mahn
apple	jabuka (f)	ya-boo-kah
approximately	približno	preeb-leezh-noh
apricots	marelice (f)	mah-re-lee-tse
arm	ruka (f)	roo-kah

English – Croatian

English - Croatian

English	Croatian	Pronunciation
to arrest	uhititi	oo-hee-tee-tee
arrivals (plane, train)	dolazak (m)	dau-lah-zahk
to arrive	doći	dau-chee
art	umjetnost (f)	oom-yet-naust
to ask (question)	pitati	pee-tah-tee
aspirin	aspirin (m)	ah-**spee**-reen
asthma	astma (f)	**ah**-stmah
at	u; kod	oo; kaud
at home	doma	dau-mah
at once	jedanput	ye-**dahn**-poot
at night	noću	**nau**-choo
to attack	napadati	nah-pah-dah-tee
attractive	privlačan(čna)	preev-**lahch**-ahn (čno)
aubergine	patlidžan (m)	pah-**tlee**-djan
Australia	Australija (f)	ow-strah-**lee**-ya
Australian	australski(a)(o)	ow-strahl-**skee**-ya
automatic	automatski(a)(o)	ow-tau-**maht**-skee
autumn	jesen (f)	**ye**-sen
available	dostupan(pna)(pno)	daus-too-pahn
to avoid	izbjeći	eez-**bye**-chee
awake: to be awake	budan(dna)(dno)	**boo**-dahn
away	daleko	**dah**-le-koh
awfully	užasno	oo-**zhah**-snoh

B

English	Croatian	Pronunciation
baby	beba (f)	beba
baby milk	mlijeko za djecu (n)	mlee-**ye**-koh zah **dye**-tsoo
baby nappies	pelene	pe-**le**-ne
babyseat (in car)	sjedalo za dijete (n)	**sye**-dah-loh zah **dee**-ye-te
baby carriage	dječja kolica (f)	dychee-ya
back (of body)	leđa (f)	**le**-djah
bad (weather, news, food)	loše	**loh**-she

English – Croatian

English	Croatian	Pronunciation
bag	torba (f)	**taur**-bah
baker's	pekarnica (f)	**peck**-ahr-nee-tsa
banana	banana (f)	**bah**-nah-nah
bank	banka (f)	**bahn**-kah
bank (river)	obala (f)	**aub**-ah-lah
banknote	novčanice (f)	**nauv**-chah-nee-tse
bar	bar (m)	bahr
basil	bosiljak (m)	**baus**-ee-lyahk
bath	kupka (f)	**koop**-kah
bathroom	kupaonica (f)	**koo**-pow-nee-tsah
battery (radio, etc)	baterija	**bah**-te-ree-yah
beach	plaža (f)	**plah**-zhah
bean	grah (m)	gr-**ah**
beautiful	lijep(a)(o)	**lee**-ye-poh
because	zato	**paus**-tah-tee
bed	krevet (m)	kre-vet
double bed	bračni krevet (m)	**bratch**-nee **kreh**-vet

Croatian	English	Pronunciation
krevet za jednu osobu (m)	*single bed*	kre-vet zah jeh-dnoo **au**-sau-boo
spavaonica (f)	bedroom	spah-**vow**-nee-tsah
Prenoćište i doručak	B&B	**pre**-nauch-**ee**-shte ee **daur**-oo-chak
biti	*to be*	**bee**-tee
pivo (n)	beer	**pee**-voh
točeno pivo (n)	draught beer	**tau**-che-noh **pee**-voh
prije	before	**pree**-ye
početi	to begin	**pau**-che-tee
iza	behind	**ee**-zah
vjerovati	to believe	**vye**-rau-vah-tee
pripadati	to belong	**pree**-pah-dah-tee
ispod	below	**ees**-paud
pokraj	beside (next to)	**pau**-kray
najbolji(a)(e)	best: *the best*	nay-**bau**-lyee
bolje no	better (than)	**bau**-lye noh
medu	between	**me**-joo

English – Croatian

English	Croatian	Pronunciation
to beware of	paziti se	**pah**-zee-tee se
beyond	izvan	**eez**-vahn
bicycle	bicikl (m)	**bee**-tsee-kl
big	veliko	**ve**-lee-koh
bigger (than)	veći nego	**ve**-chee ne-goh
bill (hotel, restaurant)	račun (m)	**rah**-choon
birthday	rođendan (m)	**rau**-jen-dahn
happy birthday!	Sretan rođendan!	**sre**-than rau-jen-dahn!
birthday card	rođendanska čestitka (f)	rau-jen-**dahn**-ska **ches**-teet-kah
birthday present	rođendanski poklon (m)	rau-jen-**dahn**-ska **pau**-cklaun
biscuits	dvopek (m)	**dvau**-peck
a bit	malo	**mah**-loh
bite (of insect)	ubod (m)	oo-**baud**
bite (of dog)	ugriz (m)	oo-**gr**-eez
bitten	uboden(a)(o)	oo-bau-de-n
bitter (taste)	gorak(rka)(rko)	**gau**-rahck
black	crn(a)(o)	tsrn
to bleed	krvariti	kr-**vah**-ree-tee
blind (person)	slijepac(pica) (m)	**slee**-ye-pahts
blond (person)	plavuša (f)	**plah**-voo-shah
blood	krv (f)	krv
blood pressure	krvni tlak (m)	kr-vnee tlahk
blouse	bluza (f)	**bloo**-zah
blue (light)	modro	**maud**-rau
boarding card/pass	karta za ulaz u avion (f)	**kahr**-tah zah oo-laz oo ah-**vee**-on
body	tijelo (n)	**tee**-ye-loh
to boil	kuhati	**koo**-h-ah-tee
book	knjiga (f)	kny-**ee**-gah
to book	rezervirati	re-zer-**vee**-rah-tee
booking office (train)	blagajna (f)	**blah**-gahy-nah
bookshop	knjižara (f)	kny-**ee**-zhah-rah
boots (long)	visoke čizme (f)	**vee**-soh-ke **cheez**-me
(ankle)	niske čizme (f)	nees-ke-**cheez**-me

English	Croatian	Pronunciation
boring	dosadan(dna) (dno)	dau-sahd-an
both	oboje	oh-boh-ye
bottle	boca (f)	bau-tsah
bottle of wine	boca vina	bau-tsa vee-nah
box office	blagajna (f)	blah-gahy-nah
boy (young child)	dječak (m)	dye-chahk
boy (teenage)	mladić (m)	mlah-deech
boyfriend	momak (m)	mau-mahk
to brake	zakočiti	zah-kau-chee-tee
brakes	kočnice (f)	kauch-nee-tse
brave	hrabar(bra)(bro)	hah-bahr
bread	kruh (m)	krooh
bread roll	pecivo (n)	pe-tsee-voh
to break	slomiti	slau-mee-tee
breakfast	zajutrak (m)	zah-yoo-track
to breathe	disati	dee-sah-tee
bride	mlada (f)	mlah-dah
bridegroom	mladoženja (m)	mlah-dau-zhe-nya
briefcase	aktovka (f)	ahk-tauv-kah
to bring	donijeti	dau-nee-ye-tee
Britain	Velika Britanija (f)	ve-lee-kah bree-tah-nee-yah
British	britanski(o)	bree-tahn-skee
broccoli	prokulica (f)	prau-koo-lee-tsah
brochure	knjižica (f)	kny-ee-zhee-tsah
broken	slomljen(a)(o)	slaum-lyen
broken down (car; etc)	kvar (m)	kvahr
brother	brat (m)	br-aht
brown	smeđ(a)(e)	sme-jee
buffet car	vagon	vah-gaun
	restoran (m)	re-stau-rahn
bulb (lightbulb)	žarulja (f)	zhah-roo-lya
bunch (of flowers)	stručak	stroo-chak
(of grapes)	cvijeća (m)	tsvee-ye-chah
bureau de change	grozd (m)	grauzd
	mjenjačnica (f)	mye-ny-ch-nee-tsa
burger	pljeskavica (f)	plye-ska-vee-tsa

burglar	provalnik (m)	pro-val-neeck
bus	autobus (m)	ow-toh-boos
bus stop	postaja (f)	paus-tahya
bus ticket	autobusna karta (f)	ow-toh-boos-kah kahr-tah
business	posao (n)	pau-sow
businessman/ woman	poslovan(vna) čovjek; žena	paus-lau-vahn chau-vyek; zhe-nna
business trip	poslovni put (m)	paus-lauv-nee poot
but	ali	ah-lee
butter	maslac (m)	mahs-lahts
to buy	kupiti	koo-pee-tee
by (next to)	uz	ooz
by bus	autobusom	ow-toh-boo-saum
by car	autom	ow-taum
by train	vlakom	vlah-kaum

C

cab (taxi)	taksi (m)	tah-ksee
café	kafe (n)	kah-vah-nah
cafetière	kafić (m)	kah-feech
cake (big)	kafetjera (f)	kah-fe-tee-yerah
cake (small)	torta (f)	taur-tah
cake shop	kolač (m)	kau-lahch
	slastičarna (f)	slah-stee-chahr-nah
call (phone call)	poziv (m)	pau-zeev
to call (phone)	zvati	zvah-tee
	telefonirati	te-le-fau-nee-rah-tee
calm	miran(rna)(mo)	mee-rahn
camcorder	videokamera (f)	vee-de-oh-kah-me-rah
camera	fotokamera (f)	fau-toh-kah-me-rah
to camp	kampirati	kam-pee-ra-tee
campsite	kamp (m)	kamp
can (to be able)	moći	mau-chee

English	Croatian	Pronunciation
Canada	Kanada (f)	kah-nah-dah
Canadian	kanadski(a)(o)	kah-nahd-skee
to cancel	opozvati	au-pauz-vah-tee
cancellation	opoziv (m)	au-pau-zeev
capital (city)	glavni grad	glah-vnee gr-ahd
car	auto (n)	ow-toh
car ferry	trajekt (m)	trah-yeckt
car hire	najam auta	na-yam ow-tah
car insurance	auto osiguranje (n)	ow-toh au-see-goo-rah-nye
car keys	ključ od auta	klyoo-tch aud ow-tah
car park	parkiralište (n)	pahr-kee-rah-leesh-te
card (greetings)	čestitka (f)	ches-teet-kah
(business)	posjetnica (f)	paus-ye-tnee-tsa
(playing cards)	igraće karte	ee-gra-che kahr-te
careful	pažljivo	pahzh-lyee-voh
carriage (railway)	vagon (m)	vah-gaun
carrots	mrkve (f)	mr-kve
to carry	nositi	naus-ee-tee
case (suitcase)	putna torba (f)	poot-nah taur-bah
cash	gotovina (f)	gau-toh-vee-nah
to cash (cheque)	unovčiti	oo-nauv-chee-tee
cash desk	blagajna (f)	blah-gay-nah
cash machine	bankomat (m)	bahn-kau-maht
castle	dvorac (m)	dvau-rahts
casualty department	hitna pomoć	heet-nah pau-mauch
cat	mačka (f)	mah-tch-kah
to catch (train, etc)	stići na vlak	stee-chee nah vlahk
cathedral	katedrala (f)	kah-te-drah-lah
Catholic	katolik (m)	kah-toh-leek
cauliflower	cvjetača (f)	tsvye-ta-tcha
celery	celer (m)	tse-ler
centimetre	centimetar (m)	tsen-tee-me-tahr
central	centralni	tsen-tr-ahl-nee
central heating	centralno grijanje	tsen-tr-ahl-nau gree-ya-nye

English – Croatian

English – Croatian

English	Croatian	Pronunciation
centre	centar (m)	tsen-tahr
century	stoljeće (n)	stau-lye-che
cereal (for breakfast)	žitne pahuljice (f)	zheet-ne pah-hoo-lye-tse
chain	lanac (m)	lah-nahts
chair	stolica (f)	stau-lee-tsah
challenge	izazov (m)	ee-zah-zauv
change (small coins)	sitniš (m)	seet-neesh
	novčići (m)	nauv-chee-che
to change money	promijeniti novac	prau-mee-ye-nee-tee nau-vahts
to change clothes	presvući se	pre-svoo-chee se
to change train	presjesti	pre-sye-stee
charge (fee)	trošak (m)	trau-shahk
charge (mobile, etc)	punjenje (f)	poo-nye-nye
cheap	jeftino	yef-tee-nau
to check	provjeriti	prauv-ye-ree-tee
to check in (airport)	prijaviti prtjagu	pree-yah-vee-tee prt-lyah-goo
(at hotel)	prijaviti se	pree-yah-vee-tee se
cheers!	živjeli!	zhee-vye-lee!
cheese	sir (m)	seer
chef	kuhar (m)	koo-hahr
chemist's	ljekarna (f)	lye-kahr-nah
cheque	ček (m)	check
cheque book	čekovna knjižica (f)	check-auv-nah knyee-zhee-tsah
cheque card	čekovna kartica (f)	check-auv-nah kahr-tee-tsah
cherries	trešnje (f)	tresh-nye
chicken	pile (n)	pee-le
chicken breast	pileća prsa	pee-le-chah pr-sah
chilli	čili (m)	tchilli
child	dijete (n)	dee-ye-te
children (small)	dječica (n)	dye-chee-tsah
(older children)	djeca	dye-tsa

English	Croatian	Pronunciation
chips (french fries)	pomfret (m)	paum-freet
chocolate	čokolada (f)	chau-kau-lah-dah
choice	izbor (m)	eez-baur
to choose	izabrati	ee-zahb-rah-tee
Christmas	Božić (m)	bau-zheech
Merry Christmas!	Sretan Božić!	bau-zheech!
church	crkva (f)	tsr-kvah
cigarette	cigarete	tsee-gah-re-te
cigarette lighter	upaljač (m)	oo-pah-lyach
cinema	kino (n)	kee-noh
circus	cirkus (m)	tseer-koos
city	grad (m)	grahd
city centre	centar grada	tsen-tahr grah-dah
class; first class	prvi razred	pr-vee rahz-red
second class	drugi razred	droo-gee rahz-red
clean	čisto	chee-stoh
clear	vedar	ve-dahr
to climb	penjati se	pe-nya-tee se
clock	ura (f)	oo-rah
closed (shop, etc)	zatvoreno	zaht-vau-re-noh
clothes	odjeća (f)	aud-ye-chah
cloudy	oblačno	aub-lach-noh
coach	autobus (m)	ow-toh-boos
coast	obala (f)	aub-ah-lah
coat	kaput (m)	kah-poot
coffee	kava (f)	kah-vah
decaffeinated coffee	kava bez kofeina	kau-vah bez kau-fe-ee-nah
cold	hladno	hlahd-noh
cold (illness)	prehlada (f)	preh-lah-dah
to collect	sakupiti	sah-koo-pee-tee
(to collect someone)	doći po nekoga	dau-chee pau ne-kaug-ah
to come (to arrive)	doći	dau-chee
to come back	vratiti se	vr-ah-tee-tee se
to come in	ući	oo-chee
comfortable	ugodno	oo-gaud-noh
complaint	prigovor (m)	pree-gau-vaur

English – Croatian

English	Croatian	Pronunciation
complete / to complete (finish)	potpun (m) / dovršiti	**paut**-poon / **dau**-vr-shee-tee
(a form)	ispuniti	**ees**-poo-nee-tee
computer	kompjutor (m)	**kaum**-pyoo-taur
concert	koncert (m)	**kaun**-tsert
concession	popust (m)	**pau**-poost
to confirm	potvrditi	**paut**-vr-dee-tee
confirmation (of flight, etc)	potvrda (f)	**paut**-vr-dah
confused	zbunjen(a)(o)	**zboo**-nyen
connection (train, etc)	presjedanje	**pres**-ye-dah-nye
consulate	konzulat (m)	**kaun**-zoo-laht
to contact	kontaktirati	**kaun**-tack-**tee**-rah-tee
contract	ugovor (m)	**oo**-gau-vaur
to cook	kuhati	**koo**-h-ah-tee
cooked	kuhan(a)(o)	**koo**-hah-noh
cookies	kolačići	**kau**-lah-chee-chee
cool	hladan(dna) (dno)	**hla**-dan
corner	ugao (m)	**oo**-gow
cornflakes	kukuruzne pahuljice	**koo**-koo-**rooz**-ne **pah**-hoo-lye-tse
corridor	hodnik (m)	**haud**-neek
cosmetics	kozmetika (f)	**kauz**-me-tee-kah
to cost	koštati	**kaush**-tah-tee
costume (swimming)	kupaći kostim (m)	**koo**-pah-chee **kaus**-teem
cough	kašalj (m)	**kah**-shahly
counter (in shop, etc)	blagajna (f)	**blah**-gahy-nah
country (not town)	zemlja (f)	**zem**-lyah
couple (two people)	država (f)	dr-**zhah**-vah
courgettes	dvoje (n)	dv-**au**-ye
	kocke šećera	**kau**-tske **she**-che-rah

English	Croatian	
course (of meal)	jelo (n)	ye-loh
(of study)	tečaj (m)	te-chay
cousin	rodak (m); rodaka (f)	rau-jack; rau-jah-kah
crafts	obrti (m)	au-br-tee
crash (car)	sudar (m)	soo-darh
to crash (car)	razbiti auto	rahz-bee-tee ow-toh
cream (lotion)	krema (f)	kre-mah
(dairy)	vrhnje (n)	vrh-nye
credit card	kreditna kartica (f)	kre-deet-nah kahr-tee-tsah
crime	zločin (m)	zlau-cheen
croissant	roščić (m)	raush-cheech
to cross (road)	prijeći ulicu	pree-ye-chee oo-lee-tsoo
crossroads	raskrsnica (f)	rahsk-r-snee-tsah
crowd	svjetina (f)	svye-tee-nah
crowded	prenatrpano (n)	pre-nah-tr-pah-noh
cucumber	krastavac (m)	krahs-tah-vahts
cup	šalica (f)	shah-lee-tsah
current	propuh (m)	prau-pooh
customer	kupac (m)	koo-pahts
to cut	odrezati	aud-re-zah-tee
to cycle	voziti bicikl	vauz-ee-tee bee-tsee-kl
cystitis	biciklist (m)	bee-tsee-kleest

D

English	Croatian	
daily (each day)	dnevno	dne-vnoh
dairy produce	mliječni proizvod	mlee-yech-nee prau-eez-vaud
damage	šteta (f)	shte-tah
damp	vlaga (f)	vlah-gah
dance	ples (m)	ples
to dance	plesati	ple-sah-tee
danger	opasnost (f)	au-pahs-naust
dangerous	opasan(sna)(sno)	au-pah-sahn
dark (colour)	taman(mna)(mno)	tah-mahn

English - Croatian

English	Croatian	Pronunciation
date	datum (m)	**dah**-toom
date of birth	datum rodenja	**dah**-toom **rau**-je-nya
daughter	kćer (f)	kcher
day	dan (m)	dahn
per day	za dan	zah **dahn**
every day	svaki dan	**svah**-kee dahn
dead	mrtav(tva)(tvo)	**mr**-tvoh
deaf	gluh	glooh
dear	draga	**drah**-gah
debts	dugovi (m)	**doo**-gau-vee
debit card	platežna kartica	**plah**-tezh-nah **kahr**-tee-tsa
deckchair	ležaljka (f)	**le**-zhah-ly-kah
to declare	prijaviti	**pree**-ya-vee-tee
deep	dubok(a)(o)	**doo**-bau-kah
delay	kasniti	**kahs**-nee-tee
delicious	ukusan(sna)(sno)	**oo**-koos-noh
dentist	zubar (m)	**zoo**-bahr
deodorant	deodorant (m)	deh-**oh**-dorant
to depart	otići	**au**-tee-chee
department store	robna kuća (f)	**raub**-nah **koo**-chah
departure	odlazak (m)	**aud**-lah-zahk
departure lounge	čekaonica	**check**-ow-nee-tsah
to describe	opisati	**au**-pee-sah-tee
description	opis (m)	**au**-pees
desk	radni stol (m)	**rahd**-nee **staul**
dessert	slatko (n)	**slaht**-koh
details	pojedinosti	**pau**-ye-dee-noh-stee
to develop (photos)	razviti slike	**rahz**-vee-tee **slee**-ke
diabetic	dijabetičar(ka)	**dee**-ya-be-tee-char
to dial	birati broj	**bee**-rah-tee **brauy**
dialling code	pozivni broj	**pau**-zeev-nee **brauy**

English	Croatian	Pronunciation
dialling tone	signal za biranje	**see**-gnahl zah **bee**-rah-nye
dictionary	rječnik (m)	**ryech**-neek
diesel	dizel	**dee**-zel
diet	dijeta	dee-**ye**-tah
different	različit(a)(o)	**rahz**-lee-cheet
difficult	težak(ška)(ško)	**tesh**-koh
digital camera	digitalna kamera (f)	dee-gee-**tahl**-nah **kah**-me-rah
dining room	blagovaonica (f)	blah-gau-**vow**-nee-tsah
dinner (evening meal)	večera (f)	**ve**-che-rah
to have dinner	večerati	ve-**che**-rah-tee
direct (train, etc)	izravan vlak	**eez**-rahv-an vlahk
directions	putokazi	**poo**-toh-kah-zee
to ask for directions	pitati za smjer	**pee**-tah-tee zah smyer
directory (telephone)	telefonski imenik	te-le-**faun**-skee **ee**-me-neek
dirty	prljavo	**prl**-ya-voh
disabled (person)	invalid (m)	een-vah-**leed**
to disagree	ne slagati se	ne **slah**-gah-tee se
to disappear	nestati	**nes**-tah-tee
disaster	udes (m)	**oo**-des
disco	disko	**dees**-koh
discount	popust (m)	**pau**-poost
to discover	otkriti	**aut**-kree-tee
disease	bolest (f)	**bau**-lest
disk (floppy disk)	disketa (f)	dee-**ske**-tah
distance	udaljenost	oodah-**lye**-nohst
district (of town)	četvrt	**tche**-tvrt
to disturb	ometati	**au**-me-tah-tee
divorced	razveden(a)	**rahz**-ve-den
to do	činiti	**tchee**-nee-tee
doctor	liječnik(ica)	lee-**yech**-neek
documents	dokumenta	dau-koo-**men**-tah
dog	pas (m)	pahs
dollars	dolari	**dau**-lah-ree
domestic (flight)	domaći let	dau-mah-**chee** let

English - Croatian

English	Croatian	pronunciation	English	Croatian	pronunciation
donor card	kartica davatelja organa (f)	**kahr**-tee-tsah dah-vah-te-lya ohr-gah-nah	drink (soft)	bezalkoholno piće (n)	bez-alkoh-olnoh **pee**-che
door	vrata (f)	**vrah**-tah	to drink	piti	**pee**-tee
double	duplo	**doop**-loh	drinking water	pitka voda (f)	**peet**kah **vau**-dah
double bed	bračni krevet	**bra**-tch-nee **kre**-vet	to drive	voziti	**vau**-zee-tee
double room	dvokrevetna soba	dvoh-**kre**-**ve**-tna **sau**-bah	driver (of car)	vozač (m)	**vau**-zahch
down: to go down	ići dolje	ee-chee **daul**-ye	driving licence	vozačka dozvola (f)	**vau**-zahch-kah **dauz**-vau-lah
downstairs	niz stepenice	**neez ste**-pe-nee-tse	to drown	ugušiti se	**oo**-goo-shee-tee se
draught (of air)	propuh (m)	**prau**-pooh	drug (medicine)	lijek (m)	**lee**-yek
draught lager	točeno pivo (n)	**tau**-che-noh **pee**-voh	drug (narcotics)	droga	droh-gah
			drunk	pijan(a)(o)	**pee**-yahn
dress	haljina (f)	**hah**-lye-nah	dry	suh(a)(o)	**soo**-h
to dress (oneself)	odjenuti se	**au**-dye-**noo**-tee se	to dry	sušiti	**soo**-shee-tee
			dry-cleaner's	kemijska čistionica	kem-**eey**-skah **chees**-teo-nee-tsah
dressing (for food)	preljev (m)	**pre**-lyev	duty-free	bez carine	bez **tsah**-ree-ne
			DVD player	DVD player	de-ve-de **ple**-yer

E

English	Croatian	Pronunciation
each	svaki	svah-kee
ear (n)	uho (n)	oo-hoo
earache	uhobolja	oo-ho-baul-yah
earlier	ranije	rah-nee-ye
early	rano	rah-noh
to earn	zaraditi	zah-rah-dee-tee
earphones	slušalice	sloo-shah-lee-tse
east	istok (m)	ee-stauk
Easter	Uskrs	oos-krs
easy	lako	lah-koh
to eat	jesti	yes-tee
egg	jaje (n)	ya-ye
fried egg	prženo jaje	pr-zhe-noh ya-ye
either	ili	ee-lee
electric	električni(a)(o)	e-lek-tree-tchnah-nee
electricity	struja (f)	stroo-yah
electric toothbrush	električna zubna četkica	e-lek-tree-tchnah zoob-nah chet-kee-tsah

English	Croatian	Pronunciation
e-mail	elektronska pošta	e-lek-traun-skah paush-tah
e-mail address	e-mail adresa	ee-meyl add-re-sah
embassy	poslanstvo (n)	paus-lahn-stvoh
emergency	hitna	heet-nah
	služba (f)	sloozh-bah
emergency exit	izlaz u opasnosti	eez-lahz oo au-pahs-naus-tee
empty	prazno	prahz-noh
end	kraj (m)	kray
engaged (to be married)	zaručen(a)	zah-roo-chen
(phone, toilet, etc)	zauzet(a)(o)	zah-oo-zet
England	Engleska	eng-les-kah
English	Englez(skinja)	en-glez(skee-nyah)
English (language)	engleski (m)	en-gle-skee
to enjoy	uživati	oo-zhee-vah-tee
(to like)	sviđati se	svee-jah-tee se
enough	dosta	daus-tah
that's enough	Sad je dosta	sahd ye daus-tah

English – Croatian

English	Croatian	Pronunciation
enquiry desk	informacije	een-**fau**-r-**mah**-tsee-ye
to enter	uči	**oo**-chee
entrance	ulaz (m)	**oo**-lahz
entrance fee	cijena ulaza (f)	**tsee**-ye-nah **oo**-lah-zah
equal	jednako	**yed**-nah-koh
equipment	oprema (f)	**aup**-re-mah
error	pogreška (f)	**paug**-resh-kah
to escape	izbjeći	eez-**bye**-chee
essential	bitan(tna)(tno)	**beet**-noh
euro	euro (n)	**e**-oo-roh
Europe	Europa (f)	e-oo-**rau**-pah
European	europsko	e-oo-**raup**-skoh
evening	večer (f)	**ve**-cher
this evening	večeras	**ve**-che-ras
tomorrow	sutra navečer	**soot**-rah nah-**ve**-cher
evening		
every	svaki(ka)(ko)	**svah**-kee
everyone	svatko (m)	**svah**-tkoh
everything	sve	sve
everywhere	svuda	**svoo**-dah
example: *for example*	na primjer	nah **pree**-myer
excellent	izvrstan(sna)(sno)	**eez**-vr-snoh
except	osim	**aus**-eem
to exchange	zamijeniti	zah-**mee**-ye-nee-tee
exchange rate	kurs	koors
exciting	uzbudljiv(a)(o)	ooz-**bood**-lyeev
to excuse	ispričati se	ees-**pree**-tcha-tee se
exercise	vježba (f)	**vyezh**-bah
exhibition	izložba (f)	eez-**lohzh**-bah
exit	izlaz (m)	**eez**-lahz
expenses	troškovi	**traush**-koh-vee
expensive	skupa(o)	skoop
to expire (ticket, etc)	nevažeći(a)(e)	ne-**vah**-zhe-chee
to explain	objasniti	**aub**-yahs-nee-tee
to export	izvoziti	**eez**-vau-zee-tee

English	Croatian	Pronunciation
express (train)	ekspresni vlak	**eks**-pres-nee vlahk
extra (spare)	suvišan(šna)(šno)	**soo**-vee-shan-she
(more)	više	**vee**-she
an extra bed	dodatni ležaj	**dau**-daht-nee le-zhahy
eye	oko (n)	**au**-koh
F		
face	lice (n)	**lee**-tse
facilities (leisure facilities)	pogodnosti (f)	**pau**-gaud-nau-stee
to faint	onesvijestiti se	au-nes-**vee**-yes-tee-tee se
fair (just)	pravedan(dna)(dno)	**pra**-veh-dan
(blond)	plavuša (f)	**plah**-voo-shah
fake	lažan(žna)(žno)	**lahzh**-nah
fall (autumn)	jesen (f)	**ye**-sen
to fall	pasti	**pah**-stee
family	obitelj (f)	**au**-bee-tely
famous	slavan(vna)(vno)	**slah**-vahn
far	daleko	**dah**-le-koh
fare	cijena (f)	**tsee**-ye-nah
fashionable	staromodan (dna)(dno)	**stah**-rau-maud-an
fast	hitar(tra)(tro)	**hee**-tar
fat	debeo (m); debela (f)	**de**-be-au; **de**-be-lah
father	otac (m)	**au**-tahts
fault (defect)	greška (m)	gre-shka
fax	faks (m)	fahks
to feel	osjećati	aus-ye-chah-tee se
feet	stopala (n)	**stau**-pah-lah
to fetch (to go and get)	dovesti	**dau**-ves-tee
	ići po nekoga	**ee**-chee pau **ne**-koh-gah
fever	vrućica (f)	**vroo**-chee-tsah
few	malo	**mah**-loh

English – Croatian

English	Croatian	Pronunciation
a few	nekolicina	ne-toh-lee-tsee-nah
fiancé(e)	zaručnik (m)	zah-rooch-neek
to fight	boriti se	bau-ree-tee see
to fill	puniti	poo-nee-tee
to fill in (in form)	ispuniti	ees-poo-nee-tee
film (at cinema)	film (m)	feelm
film (for camera)	film (m)	feelm
to find	naći	nah-chee
fine (to be paid)	kazna (f)	kahz-nah
finger	prst (m)	prst
to finish	okončati	au-kaun-chah-tee
finished	okončan(a)(o)	au-kaun-chah-n
fire	vatra (f)	vah-trah
fire alarm	znak uzbune	znahk zah
fire escape	izlaz u slučaju opasnosti	eez-lahz oo sloo-tcha-yoo au-pahs-naus-tee
fire extinguisher	vatrogasni aparat	vah-trau-gahs-nee ah-pah-raht
firm (company)	poduzeće (n)	paud-oo-ze-che
first	prvi(a)(o)	pr-voh
first aid	prva pomoć	pr-vah
first class	prvi razred	pau-mauch
first name	ime	prvee rahz-red
fish	riba (f)	ee-me
to fish	ribariti	ree-bah
to fit (clothes)	podesiti	ree-bah-ree-tee
to fix	pričvrstiti	pau-de-see-tee
fizzy	gazirano	preech-vr-stee-tee
flash (for camera)	fleš (f)	gaz-eera-noh
flat	ravno	flesh
flavour	brašno (n)	rav-noh
flesh	meso (n)	bransh-noh
flight	let (m)	me-sau
floor (of building)	kat (m)	let
floor (of room)	pod (m)	kaht
flowers	cvijeće (n)	paud
flu	gripa (f)	tsvee-ye-che
		gree-pah

to fly	letjeti	let-ye-tee
fog	magla (f)	mah-glah
foggy	maglovito	mahg-lau-vee-toh
to fold	saviti	sah-vee-tee
to follow	slijediti	slee-ye-dee-tee
food	hrana (f)	hrah-nah
food poisoning	trovanje hranom	trauva-nyeh hrah-nom
foot	stopalo (n)	stau-pah-loh
on foot	pješice	pye-shee-tse
football	nogomet (m)	nau-gau-met
for	za	zah
for me/us	za mene; za nas	zah me-ne; zah nahs
for him/her	za njega; za nju	zah nye-gah; zah nyoo
for you	za tebe (singular) za vas (plural)	zah te-be zah vahs
forbidden	zabranjen(a)(o)	zahb-rah-nye-n
foreign	stran(a)(o)	strah-noh
foreigner	stranac (m)	strah-nahts
forever	zauvijek	zah-oo-vee-yek
to forget	zaboraviti	zah-bau-rah-vee-tee
fork (for eating)	vilica (f)	vee-lee-tsah
form (document)	obrazac (m)	o-brah-zats
fortnight	za dva tjedna	zah dvah tyed-nah
forward	naprijed	nahp-ree-yed
fountain	vodoskok (m)	vau-daus-kohk
fracture	lom (m)	laum
fragile	krhak(hka)(hko)	krh-ak
free (not occupied)	slobodan(dna) (dno)	slau-baud-noh
free (costing nothing)	besplatan(tna) (tno)	bes-plaht-noh
frequent	učestao(ala) (alo)	oo-che-stah-oh
fresh	svjež(a)(e)	svyezh
Friday	petak (m)	pe-tack
fried	pečen(a)(o)	pe-chen
friend	prijatelj(ica)	pree-ya-tely
friendly	prijateljski(a)(o)	pree-ya-tely-skee

English – Croatian

English	Croatian	Pronunciation
from	iz	eez
from Scotland	iz Škotske	eez **shkaut**-skee
from England	iz Engleske	eez **en**-gle-ske
front	pročelje (n)	**prau**-che-lye
in front of...	ispred...	**ees**-pred...
fruit	voće (n)	**vau**-che
fruit juice	voćni sok (m)	**vauch**-nee sauk
to fry	pržiti	pr-**zhee**-tee
fuel (petrol)	gorivo (n)	**gau**-ree-voh
full	pun(a)(o)	poon
(occupied)	zauzet(a)(o)	**zah**-oo-zet
full board	puni pansion	**poo**-nee **pahn**-seon
fun	razonoda (f)	rah-zau-**nau**-dah
funny (amusing)	zabavan(vna)(vno)	zah-**bah**-vahn
furnished	namješten(a)(o)	nahm-**yesh**-te-noh
future	budućnost (f)	boo-**dooch**-naust

G

gallery	galerija (f)	gah-le-**ree**-ya
game	igra (f)	**eeg**-rah
garage (private)	garaža (f)	gah-**rah**-zhah
garden	vrt (m)	vrt
generous	darežljiv(a)(o)	**dah**-rezh-lyeev
gents' (toilet)	muški WC	**moo**-shkee ve-tse
genuine (leather, silver)	pravo	**prah**-voh
(antique, etc)	starinarnica (f)	**stah**-ree-**nahr**-nee-tsah
German (language)	Nijemac(ica)	**nee**-ye-mahts
German	njemački(ka)(o)	**nye**-mah-chkee
Germany	Njemačka	**nye**-mah-chkah
to get (obtain)	dobiti	**dau**-bee-tee
(to receive)	primiti	**pree**-mee-tee
to get in/on (vehicle)	doći po	**dau**-chee pau
	popeti se na	**pau**-pe-tee se na
to get off (bus, etc)	ući u	**oo**-chee oo

English – Croatian

English	Croatian	Pronunciation
gift	poklon (m)	pauk-laun
girl (young child)	djevojčica (f)	dye-**vauy**-chee-tsah
(teenage)	djevojka (f)	dye-**vauy**-kah
girlfriend	cura (f)	**tsoo**-rah
to give	dati	**dah**-tee
to give back	vratiti	**vrah**-tee-tee
glass (substance)	staklo (n)	**stahk**-loh
(for drinking)	čaša (f)	tcha-sha
a glass of water	čaša vode	**chah**-shah **vau**-de
a glass of wine	čaša vina	**chah**-shah **vee**-nah
glasses (specs)	naočale	**now**-chah-le
to go	ići	**ee**-chee
to go back	vraćati se	**vrah**-chah-tee se
to go in	ući u	**oo**-chee oo
to go out (leave)	izaći	**eez**-ah-chee
good	dobar	**dau**-bahr
(pleasant)	ugodno	**oo**-gaud-noh
very good	jako dobro	**ya**-koh **daub**-roh
good		
afternoon (after 5pm)	dobar dan	**dau**-bahr dahn
goodbye	dobra večer	**daub**-rah **ve**-cher
good day	doviđenja	**dau**-vee-**je**-nya
good evening	dobar dan	**dau**-bahr dahn
good morning	dobra večer	**daub**-rah **ve**-cher
good night	dobro jutro	**daub**-roh **yoot**-roh
gram	laku noć	**lah**-koo nauch
grandchild	gram (m)	grahm
grandparents	unuk(a)(če) (f)	**oo**-nook; **oo**-noo-kah
grapefruit	djed (m); baka (f)	dyed; **bah**-kah
grapes	grejpfrut (m)	**greyp**-froot
great (big)	grožđe (n)	**grauzh**-je
(wonderful)	velik(a)(o)	**ve**-lee-koh
Great Britain	čudesan(sna) (sno)	**choo**-des-noh
greengrocer's	Velika Britanija	**ve**-lee-kah **bree**-tah-nee-ya
	mješovita roba	**mye**-shau-vee-tah **rau**-bah

English – Croatian

English	Croatian	Pronunciation
greetings	pozdravi (m)	poz-drah-vee
grey	siv(a)(o)	**see**-vau
grilled	s roštilja	s **raush**-tee-lya
ground floor	prizemlje (n)	**pree**-zeem-lye
group	skupina (f)	**skoo**-pee-nah
guest (house guest)	gost(šća)	gaust
guest (in hotel)	turist	**too**-reest
guesthouse	kuća za goste	**koo**-chah zah **gau**-ste
guide (tourist)	turistički vodič	**too**-rees-**teech**-kee **vau**-deetch
guidebook	vodič (m)	**vau**-deech
guided tour	izlet s vodičem	**eez**-let s vau-**dee**-chem

H

English	Croatian	Pronunciation
hair	kosa (f)	**kau**-sah
hairdresser	frizer (f); brijač (m)	**freez**-er; bree-**yach**-nee-tsah
half	pola	**pau**-lah
half bottle of…	pola boce…	**pau**-lah **bau**-tse…
half an hour	pola sata	**pau**-lah **sah**-tah
half board	poludnevni boravak	**pau**-loo-dne-vnee **bau**-rah-vahk
half fare	pola cijene	**pau**-lah tsee-**ye**-neh
half-price	pola cijene	**pau**-lah tsee-**ye**-neh
ham (cooked)	kuhana šunka	**koo**-hah-nah **sun**-kah
(cured)	pršut (m)	pr-**shoot**
hamburger	pljeskavica (f)	plye-skah-**vee**-tsah
hand	ruka (f)	**roo**-kah
handkerchief	rupčić (m)	**roop**-tcheech
handlebars	rukohvati (m)	**roo**-kau-h-**vah**-tee
hand luggage	ručna prtljaga	**rootch**-nah prt-**lyah**-gah
handsome	naočit(a)(o)	now-**tcheet**
to happen	dogoditi se	**dau**-gau-dee-tee se

English	Croatian	Pronunciation
what happened?	Što se dogodilo?	**shtoh** se **dau**-gau-dee-loh?
happy	sretno	**sret**-noh
happy	Sretan	**sre**-tahn
birthday!	Sretan rođendan!	**rau**-jen-dahn!
hard (difficult)	tvrd(a)(o)	**tvr**-dau
to have	teško	**tesh**-koh
head	imati	**ee**-mah-tee
headache	glava (f)	**glah**-vah
health	glavobolja (f)	**glah**-vau-bau-lya
healthy	zdravlje (n)	**zdrahv**-lye
to hear	zdravo	**zdrah**-vau
heart	čuti	**choo**-tee
to heat up (food)	srce (n)	srtse
heating	podgrijati	**paud**-gree-ya-tee
heavy	hranu	**hrah**-noo
height	grijanje (n)	**gree**-ya-nye
hello! (on telephone)	težak(ška)(ško)	te-**zhee**-nah
	težina (f)	bauk!
	bok!	hah-loh
	halo	

English	Croatian	Pronunciation
help!	Upomoć!	**oo**-pau-mauch!
to help	pomoći	**pau**-mau-chee
her	njezin(a)(o)	**nye**-zee-noh
her passport	njena putovnica	**nye**-nah poo-**tauv**-nee-tsah
her room	njena soba	**nye**-nah **sau**-bah
here	ovdje	auv-dye
here is...	tu je...	too ye...
to hide	sakriti	**sah**-kree-tee
high (speed)	visok(a)(o)	**vee**-sau-koh
	velika brzina	**ve**-lee-kah br-**zee**-nah
him	njemu; njega	**nye**-moo; **nye**-gah
hire	najam (m)	**nah**-yahm
car hire	unajmiti auto	**oo**-nahy-mee-tee **ow**-toh
his	njegov(a)(o)	**nye**-gau-vau
his passport	njegova putovnica	**nye**-gau-vah poo-**tauv**-nee-tsah

English – Croatian

English – Croatian

English	Croatian	Pronunciation
his room	njegova soba	nye-gau-vah sau-bah
historic	povijesni(a)(o)	pau-vee-yes-nee
hobby	hobi (m)	hau-bee
to hold	držati	dr-zhah-tee
(to contain)	sadržavati	sah-dr-zhah-vah-tee
hold-up (traffic)	zadržavati	zah-dr-zhah-vah-tee
holiday	blagdan; praznik (m)	blahg-dahn; prahz-neek
on holiday	na odmoru	nah aud-mau-roo daum
home	dom (m)	dau-mah
at home	doma	dau-mah
honest	iskren(a)(o)	ees-kre-nah
to hope	nadati se	nah-dah-tee se
hospital	bolnica (f)	baul-nee-tsah
hot	vruć(a)(e)	vroo-che
hotel	hotel (m)	hau-tel
hour	sat (m)	saht
	kuća (f)	koo-chah

English	Croatian	Pronunciation
house wine	domaće vino	dau-mah-che vee-noh
how? (in what way)	Na koji način?	nah kau-ye nah-cheen?
how much?	Koliko puno?	kau-lee-koh poo-nau?
how many?	Koliko mnogo?	kau-lee-koh mnau-gau?
how are you?	Kako ste?	kah-koh ste?
hungry; to be hungry	biti gladan (dna)(dno)	bee-tee glah-dahn
to hurt	ozljediti	auz-lee-ye-dee-tee
that hurts	To boli!	toh bau-lee!
husband	muž; suprug (m)	moozh; soop-roog

English	Croatian	Pronunciation
I	ja	ya
ice	led (m)	led
ice cream	sladoled (m)	slah-dau-led
iced coffee	ledena kava	le-denah kah-vah

English	Croatian	Pronunciation
iced tea	ledeni čaj	le-de-nee tchay
ice lolly	sladoled na štapiću	slah-do-led nah shta-pee-choo
idea	ideja (f)	ee-de-ya
identity card	osobna iskaznica	oo-saub-nah ees-kahz-nee-tsah
if	ako	ah-koh
ill	bolestan(sna) (sno)	bau-les-tahn
illness	bolest (f)	bau-lest
immediately	odmah	aud-mah-h
to import	uvoziti	oo-vau-zee-tee
important	važan(žna)(žno)	vah-zhahn
impossible	nemoguće	ne-mau-goo-che
to improve	poboljšati	pau-bauly-shah-tee
in	u	oo
in front of	ispred	ees-pred
included	uračunat(a)(o)	oo-rah-choo-nah-toh

English	Croatian	Pronunciation
inconvenient	nezgodan(dna)(dno)	ne-zgo-dnoh
to increase	povećati	pau-ve-chah-tee
indoors	unutra	oo-noo-trah
infection	zaraza (f)	zah-rah-zah
information	obavijest (f)	au-bah-vee-yest
ingredients	sastojci (m)	sas-toy-tsee
to injure	ozlijediti	auz-lee-ye-dee-tee
injured	ozlijeden(a)(o)	auz-lee-ye-je-nah
inquiries	zamolbe (f)	zah-maul-be
insect	insekt (m)	een-seckt
inside	unutra	oo-noo-trah
instead of	umjesto	oom-yes-toh
insurance	osiguranje (n)	aus-ee-goo-rah-nye
insurance certificate	potvrda o osiguranju	paut-vr-dah au aus-ee-goo-rahny
to insure	potvrditi	paut-vr-dee-tee

English – Croatian

English – Croatian

English	Croatian	Pronunciation		English	Croatian	Pronunciation
insured: to be insured	osigurana (f); osiguran (m)	au-see-goo-rah-nah; au-see-goo-rahn		Italian (language)	talijanski(a)(o); talijanski jezik	tah-**lee**-yahn-skee; tah-lee-**yahn**-skee **ye**-zeek
interesting	zanimljiv(a)(o)	zah-neem-**lyeev** (a)(o)		Italy	Italija (f)	ee-tah-**lee**-ya
international	međunarodni (a)(o)	me-joo-**nah**-raud-nee				
into	u	oo		jacket	jakna (f)	**yak**-nah
into town	u grad	oo grahd		jam (food)	pekmez (m)	jem
into the centre	u centar grada	oo **tsen**-tahr grah-dah		jar (honey, jam, etc)	staklenka (f)	**sta**-klen-kah
to introduce	predstaviti	pred-**stah**-vee-tee		jealous	ljubomoran	**lyoo**-bau-**maur**-an
someone	nekog	**ne**-kaug		jeweller's	draguljar (m)	**drah**-goo-lyar
invitation	poziv (m)	**pau**-zeev		jewellery	dragulji (m)	**drah**-goo-lyee
to invite	pozvati	**pauz**-vah-tee		Jewish	židovski(a)(o)	**zheed**-auv-skee
Ireland	Irska	**eer**-skah		job	posao (n)	**pau**-sow
Irish	irski(a)(o)	**eer**-skee		to join (club)	upisati se	oo-pee-**sah**-tee se
iron (for clothes)	glačalo (n)	**glah**-cha-loh		to joke	šaliti se	**shah**-lee-tee se
is	je	ye		journalist	novinar (ka)	**nau**-vee-nahr
island	otok (m)	**au**-tauk		journey	putovanje (n)	poo-tau-**vah**-nye

English	Croatian	Pronunciation
to jump	skočiti	skau-tchee-tee
just just two	samo dva	sah-mau dvah

K

English	Croatian	Pronunciation
to keep (retain)	zadržati	zah-dr-**znah**-tee
key	ključ (m)	klyootch
card key	kartica ključ	**kahr**-tee-tsah klyootch
to kill	ubiti	oo-bee-tee
kilo	kila (f)	**kee**-lah
kilogram	kilogram (m)	kee-laug-rahm
kilometre	kilometar (m)	kee-lau-me-tahr
kind (sort)	vrsta (f)	vrstah
kind (person)	dobra osoba	dobrah **aus**-au-bah
kiosk	kiosk (m)	kee-ausk
to knock (door)	kucati	koo-tsah-tee
to know (facts)	znati	**znah**-tee
(to be acquainted with)	biti upoznat (a)(o) sa	**bee**-tee oo-pauz-nahtsah
to know how to	znati kako	**znah**-tee **kah**-koh
to know how to	znati	**znah**-tee
to know how to swim	plivati	**plee**-vah-tee

L

ladies' (toilet)	ženski WC	**zhen**-skee ve-tse
lady	gospoda (f)	**gaus**-pau-jah
lager	pivo (n)	**pee**-voh
lamb	janje (n)	**yah**-nye
lamp	lampa (f)	**lahm**-pah
to land (plane)	sletjeti	**sle**-tye-tee
language	jezik (m)	**yez**-eek
large	velik(a)(o)	**ve**-lee-kee
last	posljednji(a)(e)	**paus**-lyed-nye
last night	prošla noć	**praush**-lah nauch
last week	prošli tjedan	**praush**-lee **tye**-dahn
last year	prošla godina	**praush**-lah **gaud**-ee-nah
late	kasni(a)(o)	**kahs**-noh
later	kasnije	**kahs**-nee-ye

English – Croatian

English	Croatian	Pronunciation
to laugh	smijati se	smee-yah-tee se
lavatory	zahod (m)	zah-aud
lazy	lijen	lee-yen
to learn	spoznati	spauz-nah-tee
leather	koža (f)	kau-zhah
to leave (leave behind)	ostaviti iza	aus-tah-vee-tee ee-zah
(train, bus, etc)	izaći iz vlaka	eez-ah-chee eez vlah-kah
left	lijevo	lee-ye-voh
on/to the left	na lijevo	nah lee-ye-voh
left-luggage	izgubljena prtljaga	eez-goo-blye-nah prt-lyah-ga
leg	noga (m)	nau-gah
lemon	limun (m)	lee-moon
lemonade	limunada (f)	lee-moo-nah-dah
to lend	posuditi	pau-soo-dee-tee
length	dužina (f)	doo-zhee-nah
lens (camera)	leća (f)	lecha
(contact lens)	kontaktne leće	kaun-tackt-ne le-che
less	manje	mah-nye
less than	manje no	mah-nye nau
lesson	poduka (f)	pau-doo-kah
to let (allow)	dopustiti	dau-poos-tee-tee
(to hire out)	iznajmiti	eez-nahy-mee-tee
letter	pismo (n)	pees-mau
licence (driving)	dozvola (f)	dauz-vau-lah
	vozačka dozvola	vau-zatch-kah dauz-vau-lah
to lie	lagati	lah-gah-tee
lie (untruth)	laž (f)	lahzh; (ne-ees-tee-nah)
to lie down	slagati	slah-gah-tee
lift (elevator)	dizalo (n)	dee-zah-loh
light (not heavy)	lagan(a)(o)	lah-gah-nah
(colour)	svijetla boja	svee-yet-lah bau-ya
light	svjetlo (n)	svyet-loh

English	Croatian	Pronunciation
like (comparison)	kao	kow
to like	sviđati se	svee-**jah**-tee se
line (row, queue)	red (m)	red
line (telephone)	telefonska linija	te-le-**faun**-skah lee-**nee**-ya
liqueur (m)	liker (m)	**lee**-ker
list	popis (m)	**poh**-pees
to listen (to)	slušati	**sloo**-shah-tee
litre	litra (f)	**lee**-trah
litre of milk	litra mlijeka	**lee**-trah mlee-**ye**-kah
little (small)	malen(a)(o)	**mah**-len
a little...	malo...	**mah**-loh
to live	živjeti	**zhee**-vye-tee
local	mjesni(a)(o)	**myes**-nee
to lock	zaključati	zahk-**lyoo**-tchah-tee
long	dug(a)(o)	**doo**-gah
for a long time	za dugo vrijeme	zah **doo**-gau **vree**-ye-me
to look after	brinuti se	**bree**-noo-tee se
to look at	gledati	**gle**-dah-tee
to look for	tražiti	**trah**-zhee-tee
to lose	izgubiti	eez-**goob**-bee-tee
lost (object)	izgubljena stvar	eez-goob-**lye**-nah **stvahr**
lost property office	Ured za izgubljene stvari	oo-red zah eez-goob-**lye**-ne **stvah**-ree
lot: a lot	mnogo (countable); puno (uncountable)	**mnau**-gau; **poo**-noh
loud	glasno	**glahs**-noh
lounge (in hotel)	foaje (m)	fau-ah-**yeh**
lounge (in airport)	čekaonica (f)	tche-**kow**-nee-tsah
love	ljubav (f)	**lyoo**-bahv
to love (person)	voljeti	**vau**-lye-tee
lovely	krasan(sna)(sno)	**krahs**-an

English – Croatian

low - mild

English	Croatian	Pronunciation		English	Croatian	Pronunciation
low (standard, quality)	nizak(ska)(sko)	**nees**-koh		main course (meal)	glavno jelo	**glahv**-noh **ye**-loh
	niski standard	**nees**-kee **stahn**-dahr-rd		to make (generally)	načiniti	**nah-tchee**-nee-tee
to lower volume	stišati	**stee-sha-tee**		make-up (meal)	spremiti	**spre**-mee-tee
luck	sreća (f)	**sre**-chah			obrok	**aub**-rock
lucky	imati sreće	ee-mah-tee **sre**-che		make-up	šminka (f)	**shmee**-nkah
luggage	prtljaga (f)	prt-**lyah**-gah		male	muški(a)(o)	**moo**-shkee
luggage trolley	kolica za prtljagu			man	čovjek (m)	**tchau**-vyek
lunch	ručak (m)	**roo**-tchahk		to manage (be in charge of)	upravljati	oop-**rahv**-lyah-tee
				manager	upravnik (m)	oop-**rahv**-neek
M				many	mnogo	mnau-gau
machine	stroj (m)	strauy		map (of country)	zemljopisna karta	**zem**-lyau-**pees**-nah **kahr**-tah
mad (insane)	lud(a)(o)	**loo**-doh		(city)	plan grada	**plahn grah**-dah
mad (angry)	ljut(a)(o)	lyoot		marmalade	marmelada (f)	**mahr**-me-**lah**-dah
magazine	časopis (m)	**tchah**-sau-pees		married	udana (f); oženjen (m)	**oo**-dah-nah; **au**-zhe-nyen
maid (in hotel)	sobarica (f)	**sau**-bah-ree-tsah				
mail	pošta (f)	**paush**-tah				
main	glavni(a)(o)	**glahv**-nee				

English	Croatian	Pronunciation
marry: to get married	udati se; oženiti se	oo-**dah**-tee se; au-zhe-**nee**-tee se
material	materijal (m)	mah-te-**ree**-yahl
mayonnaise	majoneza (f)	mah-yau-**nee**-zah
me	meni; mene	**me**-nee; **me**-ne
meal	obrok (m)	**aub**-rauk
to mean (signify)	značiti	**znah**-tchee-tee
what does it mean?	Što to znači?	**shtoh** toh **znah**-tchee?
to measure	mjeriti	**mye**-ree-tee
meat	meso (n)	**me**-sau
medicine	lijek (m)	**lee**-yek
Mediterranean	Mediteran	me-dee-**te**-rahn
medium rare (steak)	srednje pečen	**sred**-nye **pe**-tchen
to meet	sresti	**sre**-stee
to melt	otopiti	au-toh-**pee**-tee
memory	sjećanje (n)	**sye**-chah-nye
memory (memories)	uspomene (f)	oos-pau-**me**-ne
men	ljudi (m)	**lyoo**-dee

English	Croatian	Pronunciation
to mend	popraviti	paup-**rah**-vee-te
menu	jelovnik (m)	**ye**-lauv-neek
set menu	odrediti jelovnik	**aud**-re-dee-tee **ye**-lauv-neek
message	poruka (m)	pau-**roo**-kah
metre	metar (m)	**me**-tahr
metro (underground)	podzemna Željeznica	paud-**zem**-nah **zhe**-lye-**znee**-tsah
metro station	kolodvor (m)	kau-**laud**-vaur
midday	podne (n)	**paud**-ne
at midday	u podne	oo **paud**-ne
middle	sredina	sre-**dee**-nah
middle-aged	srednjovječan (m); srednjovječna (f)	**sred**-nyau-**vye**-tchah; **sred**-nyau-**vyetch**-nah
midnight	ponoć (f)	**pau**-nauch
at midnight	u ponoć	oo **pau**-nauch
mild	blag(a)(o)	blahg

English – Croatian

English	Croatian	Pronunciation
milk	mlijeko (n)	mlee-ye-koh
fresh milk	svježe mlijeko	svye-zhe mlee-ye-koh
with milk	s mlijekom	sah mlee-ye-kaum
without milk	bez mlijeka	bez mlee-ye-kah
millimetre	milimetar (m)	mee-lee-me-tahr
mineral water	mineralna voda	mee-ne-rahl-nah vau-dah
minimum	minimum (m)	mee-nee-moom
minute	minuta (f)	mee-noo-tah
to miss (train, etc)	zakasniti na vlak	zah-kahs-nee-tee nah vlahk
Miss	gospodica	gaus-pau-je-tsa
missing (thing)	nedostaje	ne-dau-stah-ye
missing (person)	nestala osoba	ne-sta-la au-sau-bah
mistake	pogreška (f)	paug-resh-kah
to mix	pomiješati	pau-mee-ye-shah-tee
mobile phone	mobilni (m)	mau-beel-nee

English	Croatian	Pronunciation
mobile	mobilnog	mau-beel-naug
number	broj	brauy
modern	suvremeno	soov-re-me-noh
moment: just a moment	samo trenutak	sah-moh tre-noo-tack
Monday	ponedjeljak (m)	pau-ned-ye-lyahk
money	novac (m)	nau-vahts
month	mjesec (m)	mye-sets
this month	ovaj mjesec	au-vahy mye-sets
last month	prošli mjesec	praush-lee mye-sets
next month	iduči mjesec	ee-doo-chee mye-sets
more (than)	više no	vee-she nau
morning	jutro (n)	yoo-trau
in the morning	ujutro	oo-yoo-trau
this morning	jutros	yoot-raus
tomorrow morning	sutra ujutro	soo-trah oo-yoo-trau
most	većina (f)	ve-chee-nah

mother	majka (f)	**may**-kah
motor	stroj (m)	strauy
motorbike	motorkotač (m)	mau-taur-**kau**-tatch
motorway	autocesta (f)	ow-toh-**tse**-stah
mouth	usta (f)	**oos**-tah
move	pokret (m)	**pauk**-ret
movie	film (m)	feelm
Mr	gospodin (m)	gaus-**pau**-deen
Mrs	gospoda (f)	gaus-**pau**-jah
Miss	gospodica (f)	gaus-pau-**jee**-tsah
Ms	gospodična (f)	gaus-pau-**deetch**-nah
much	mnogo	**mnau**-gau
too much	previše	**pre**-vee-she
muddy (ground)	blatan(tna)(tno)	**blaht**-noh
muscle	mišić (m)	**mee**-sheech
museum	muzej (m)	**moo**-zey
music	glazba (f)	**glahz**-bah
must (to have to)	morati	**mau**-rah-tee

my	moj(a)(e)	moy
my passport	moja putovnica	**mau**-yah poo-**tauv**-nee-tsah
my room	moja soba	**mau**-yah **sau**-bah

N

name	ime (n)	**ee**-me
narrow	usko	**oos**-koh
national	nacionalni	nah-tseo-**nahl**-nee
nationality	državljanstvo (f)	dr-zha-**vlya**-nstvo
natural	prirodan(dna)(dno)	**pree**-raud-noh
nature	priroda (f)	**pree**-rau-dah
near to	blizu	**blee**-zoo
near the bank	blizu banke	**blee**-zoo **bahn**-ke
necessary	neophodan (dna)(dno)	ne-au-p-**haud**-noh
to need	trebati	**tre**-**bah**-tee
never	nikad	**nee**-kahd

English – Croatian

English – Croatian

English		Croatian	
new		nova	**nau**-vah
news		vijesti (f)	vee-**yes**-tee
news (television)		dnevnik (m)	**dnev**-neek
newspaper		novine (f)	**nau**-vee-nah
newsstand		kiosk	**kee**-ohsk
New Year		Nova Godina	**nau**-vah
Happy New Year!		Sretna Nova Godina!	**sret**-nah **nau**-vah **gau**-dee-nah!
next		sljedeći	**slye**-de-chee
next to		uz	ooz
next week		idući tjedan	**ee**-doo-chee **tye**-dahn
the next bus		idući autobus	**ee**-doo-chee **ow-toh**-boos
nice		krasno	**krah**-snau
nice (person)		ljubazna osoba	**lyoo**-bahz-nah **au**-sau-bah
niece		ljupko	**lyoop**-koo
night		noć (f)	nauch

at night		noću	**nau**-choo
last night		nocás; sinoc	**nau**-chas; see-noch
tonight		večeras	ve-**tche**-rahs
no		ne	ne
no entry		nema ulaza	**ne**-mah
no smoking		pušenje zabranjeno	**oo**-lah-zah **poo**-she-nye zah-**bra**-nye-noh
no thanks		ne hvala	ne **hvah**-lah
(without)		bez	bez
no sugar		bez šećera	bez **she**-che-rah
nobody		nitko (m)	**neet**-koh
noise		buka (f)	**boo**-kah
noisy		bučan(čna)(čno)	**bootch**-nau
non-alcoholic		bezalkoholan (lna)(lno)	**bez**-ahl-koh-hol-noh
none		nijedan(dna) (dno)	**nee**-ye-dahn
north		sjever (m)	**sye**-ver
Northern		Sieverna Irska	**sye**-ver-nah

English	Croatian	Pronunciation
Ireland		eer-skah
nose	nos (m)	naus
not	ne	ne
nothing	ništa	neesh-tah
nothing else	ništa više	neesh-tah vee-she
notice	bilješka (f)	bee-lye-shkah
now	sad	sahd
nowhere	nigdje	neeg-dye
number	broj (m)	brauy
O		
to obtain	nabaviti	nah-bah-vee-tee
odd (strange)	čudan(dna)(dno)	tchood-noh
of	od	aud
a glass of water	čaša vode	tchah-shah vau-de
made of...	načinjeno od...	nah-tchee-nye-noh aud...
office	ured (m)	oo-red

English	Croatian	Pronunciation
often	često	tches-toh
how often?	Koliko često?	kau-lee-koh tche-stoh?
OK!	U redu!	oo re-doo!
old	star(a)(o)	stahr; stah-rah
how old are you?	Koliko ste stari?	kau-lee-koh ste stah-ree?
I'm ... years old	Ja imam ... godina	ya ee-mah ... gau-dee-nah
once	jedanput	ye-dahn-poot
at once	odjednom	aud-yed-naum
only	samo	sah-moh
open	otvoren(a)(o)	aut-vau-re-noh
opposite	nasuprot	nah-soop-raut
or	ili	ee-lee
orange (colour)	narančast (a)(o)	nah-rahn-tchah-stah
orange (fruit)	naranča (f)	nah-rahn-tcha
orange juice	narančada (f)	nah-rahn-tchah-dah
order	redoslijed (m)	re-daus-lee-yed

English – Croatian

English	Croatian	Pronunciation
out of order	ne radi	
to order (food, etc)	naručiti hranu	nah-roo-tchee-tee hrah-noo
organic (food)	biološki(a)(o)	bee-oh-lau-shko
to organize	organizirati	aur-gah-nee-zee-rah-tee
others	ostali (m)	aus-tah-lee
our	naš(a)(e)	nah-she
over (on top of)	preko	pre-koh
to overbook	prebukirati	pre-boo-kee-ra-tee
to overcharge	prenaplatiti	pre-nah-pla-tee-tee
overdone (food)	prepečeno; prekuhano	pre-peh-tche-noh; pre-koo-ha-noh
to owe	dugovati	doo-gau-vah-tee

P

English	Croatian	Pronunciation
package	paket (m)	pah-cket
package tour	paket aranžman	pah-cket a-ran-zhman
page	stranica (f)	strah-nee-tsah
paid	plaćen(a)(o)	plah-che-nau
pain	bol (f)	baul
painful	bolan(lna)(lno)	baul-nau
painting (picture)	slika (f)	slee-kah
pair	par (m)	pahr
palace	palača (f)	pah-lah-tchah
pale	blijed(a)(o)	blee-ye-dah
paper	papir (m)	pah-peer
parcel	paket (m)	pah-cket
pardon?	Oprostite?	oup-raus-tee-te?
I beg your pardon!	Ispričavam se!	ee-spree-tcha-vam se!
parents	roditelji (m)	rau-dee-te-lye
park	park (m)	pahrk
to park	parkirati	pahr-kee-rah-tee
parmesan	parmezan (m)	pahr-me-zahn
part	dio (m)	deeo
partner (business)	poslovni partner	paus-lauv-nee pahrt-ner
party	proslava (f);	proh-slava;

English	Croatian	Pronunciation
(celebration)	tulum (m)	too-loom
passenger	putnik (m)	poot-neek
passport	putovnica (f)	poo-tauv-neet-sah
pastry	kolač (m)	kau-latch
to pay	platiti	plah-tee-tee
I want to pay	Želim platiti	zhe-leem plah-tee-tee
where do I pay?	Gdje ću platit?	gd-ye choo plah-tee-tee?
peace	mir (m)	meer
peaches	breskve (f)	bres-kve
pears	kruške (f)	kroosh-ke
peas	grašak (m)	grah-shahk
to peel (fruit)	guliti	goo-lee-tee
pen	olovka (f)	oh-lauv-kah
pensioner	umirovljenik (ica)	oo-mee-rauv-lye-neek
people	ljudi (m)	lyoo-dee
pepper (spice)	papar (m)	pah-pahr
pepperoni	ljute paprike	lyoo-te pahp-ree-ke
per	na; za	nah; zah
per day	na; dan	nah; dahn
per week	tjedno	tye-dnoh
per person	po osobi	pau aus-au-bee
performance	predstava (f)	pred-stah-vah
perhaps	možda	mauzh-dah
person	osoba (f)	aus-au-bah
petrol	gorivo (n)	gau-ree-voh
petrol station	benzinska crpka	ben-zeen-skah tsr-pkah
pharmacy	ljekarna (f)	lye-kahr-nah
phone	telefon (m)	te-le-faun
by phone	telefonom	te-le-fau-naum
to phone	telefonirati	te-le-fau-nee-rah-tee
phonebox	telefonska kabina	te-le-faun-skah kah-bee-nah
phonecard	telefonska kartica	te-le-faun-skah kahr-tee-tsah
to photocopy	fotokopirati	fau-toh-koh-

English - Croatian

English – Croatian

English	Croatian	Pronunciation
		...pee-rah-tee
photograph	fotograf (m)	fau-toh-grahf
to take a photo	snimiti	snee-mee-tee
phrasebook	knjiga fraza	knyee-gah frah-zah
to pick (fruit, flowers)	brati	brah-tee
(to choose)	izabrati	ee-zah-brah-tee
piece	komad (m)	koh-mahd
pillow	jastuk	yahs-took
pink	ružičasto	roo-zhee-tchah-stau
pity: *what a pity!*	Kakva šteta!	kah-kvah shte-tah!
pizza	pica (m)	pee-tsah
place	mjesto (m)	mye-stoh
place of birth	mjesto rodenja	mye-stoh rau-je-nyah
plan	plan (m)	plahn
to plan	planirati	plah-nee-rah-tee
plane	avion	ah-veeon
	zrakoplov (m)	zrah-koh-plauv
plastic (made of)	plastično	plahs-teech-nau
platform (railway)	peron (m)	pe-raun
from which platform?	S kojeg perona?	s kau-yeg pe-rauna?
play (theatre)	predstava (f)	pred-stah-vah
to play (games)	igrati	eeg-rah-tee
pleasant	ugodan(dna) (dno)	oo-gaud-nau
please	molim; izvolite	mau-leem; eez-vau-lee-te
pleased to meet you!	Drago mi je!	drah-gau mee ye!
plum	šljiva (f)	shlyee-vah
poached (egg)	obaren(a)(o)	oh-bah-reh-noh
pocket	džep (m)	jep
point	točka (f)	tauch-kah
poisonous	otrovan(vna) (vno)	au-trauv-noh
police	policija (f)	pau-lee-tsee-ya
police station	policiiska	pau-lee-tseey-

polluted	zagađen(a)(o) (m)	zah-gah-je-noh
pool (swimming)	bazen (m)	bah-zen
poor	siromašan (šna)(šno)	see-rau-mahsh-noh
pork	svinjetina (f)	svee-nye-tee-nah
porter (for luggage)	nosač (m)	naus-ahtch
	nosač prtljage	naus-ahch prt-**lyah**-ge
possible	moguće	mau-**goo**-che
post: by post	poštom	**paush**-taum
to post (letters)	poslati	paus-**lah**-tee
postbox	poštanski sanducić	**paush**-tahn-skee sahn-doo-tchech
postcard	razglednica (f)	rahz gle-**dnee**-tsah
postcode	broj pošte (m)	brauy **paush**-te
post office	pošta (f)	**paush**-tah
to postpone	odgoditi	aud-**gau**-dee-tee
potato	krumpir (m)	**kroom**-peer
pound (money)	funta (f)	**foon**-tah

to pour	natočiti	nah-**tau**-tchee-tee
power (electricity)	struja (f)	**stroo**-yah
to prefer:	više volim...	**vee**-she
I prefer...		**vau**-leem...
prescription	pripremiti	pree-**pre**-mee-tee
	recept (m)	re-**tsept**
present (gift)	poklon; dar (m)	**pauk**-laun; dahr
pretty	zgodan(dna) (dno)	**zgau**-dan
price	cijena (f)	**tsee**-ye-nah
price list	cjenovnik (m)	**tsye**-nauv-neek
private	osoban(bna) (bno)	**aus**-aub-an
probably	vjerojatno	vye-rau-yat-nau
problem	problem (m)	**praub**-lem
prohibited	zabranjen(a)(o)	zah-brah-**nye**-n
promise	obećanje (n)	au-bech-**ah**-nye
to promise	obećati	au-**bech**-ah-tee
to pronounce	izgovariti	eez-gau-vau-ree-tee
to provide	snabdjeti	**snahb**-dye-tee

English – Croatian

English	Croatian	Pronunciation
public	javnost (f)	**yahv**-naust
public holiday	praznik (m)	**prahz**-neek
pudding	slatko (n)	**slaht**-koh
to pull	povući	**pau**-voo-chee
purple	ljubičast(a)(o)	**lyoo**-bee-tchah-stau
purse	novčanik (m)	nauv-tchah-neek
to push	gurati	**goo**-rah-tee
to put (to place)	staviti	**stah**-vee-tee
pyjamas	pidžama (f)	**pee**-dja-mah

Q

English	Croatian	Pronunciation
quality	kvaliteta (f)	kvah-**lee**-teh-tah
quantity	količina (f)	kau-**lee**-tchee-nah
to quarrel	svađati se	svah-**jah**-tee-se
quarter: a quarter	četvrt (f)	**tche**-tvrt
question	pitanje (n)	**pee**-tah-nye
queue	red (m)	red
to queue	čekati u redu	**tche**-kah-tee oo **re**-doo

English	Croatian	Pronunciation
quick	hitar(tra)(tro)	**hee**-tahr
quickly	hitro	**hee**-trau
quiet (place)	tiho mjesto	**tee**-hau **mye**-stau
a quiet room	tiha soba	**tee**-hah **sau**-bah
quite (rather)	naročito	**nah**-rau-tchee-toh

R

English	Croatian	Pronunciation
race (sport)	trka (f)	tr-kah
racket (tennis)	reket (m)	**re**-ket
radio	radio (n)	**rah**-dee-oh
railway station	kolodvor (m)	**kau**-laud-vaur
rain	kiša (f)	**kee**-shah
to rain	kišiti	**kee**-shee-tee
it's raining	kiša pada	**kee**-shah **pah**-dah
raincoat	kišni kaput	**keesh**-nee **kah**-poot
raped	silovan(a) (f)	**see**-lau-vah-n/ah
rare (unique)	rijedak(tka)(tko)	**ree**-ye-dahk
raspberries	maline (f)	**mah**-lee-ne

rate (cost)	cijena (f)	tsee-ye-nah	to reduce	umanjiti	oo-**mah**-nyee-tee
rate of exchange	kurs (m)	koors	to refuse	odbiti	**aud**-bee-tee
raw	sirov(a)(o)	see-rau-vau	regarding	u pogledu	oo **paug**-le-doo
razor	britva (f)	breet-vah	region	oblast (f)	**aub**-lahst
to read	čitati	tchee-tah-tee	register (m)	registar (m)	**reh**-gee-stahr
ready	spreman(mna) (mno)	spre-mnau	registration form	prijavni list	**pree**-yahv-nee leest
to get ready	pripremiti se	pree-**pre**-mee-tee se	relation (family)	obiteljski odnosi	**aub**-ee-tely-skee **aud**-nau-see
real	stvaran(rna) (rno)	**stvah**-rahn	relationship	prijateljstvo (n)	pree-yah-**tely**-stvau
to realize	ostvariti	aus-**tvah**-ree-tee	to remain	ostati	**aus**-tah-tee
receipt	račun (m)	**rah**-tchoon	to remember	pamtiti	**pahm**-tee-tee
reception (desk)	recepcija (f)	re-**tse**-ptsee-yah	I don't remember	Ne sjećam se	ne sye-cham se
receptionist	recepcioner (ka)	re-**tsep**-tsee-**auner**	to remove	ukloniti	ooh-**klau**-nee-tee
to recognize	prepoznati	pre-**pau**-znah-tee	repair	popravak (m)	**paup**-rah-vahk
to recommend	preporučiti	pre-pau-**roo**-tchee-tee	to repair	popraviti	**paup**-rah-vee-tee
red	crven(a)(o)	tsr-**ve**-nau	to repeat	ponoviti	pau-**nau**-vee-tee
			to reply	odgovoriti	**aud**-gau-**vau**-ree-tee

English – Croatian   206 | 207

English - Croatian

English	Croatian	Pronunciation
to report (crime)	prijaviti (m)	pree-**ya**-vee-tee
request	zahtjev (m)	**zah**-htyev
to request	zatražiti	zah-**trah**-zhee-tee
reservation	rezervacija (f)	re-zer-**vah**-tsee-ya
to reserve	rezervirati	re-zer-**vee**-rah-tee
reserved	rezerviran(a)(o)	re-zer-**vee**-rah-nau
rest (repose)	odmor (m)	**aud**-maur
to rest	odmoriti se	aud-**mau**-ree-tee se
restaurant	restoran (m)	res-**tau**-rahn
restaurant car	restoran vagon	res-**tau**-rahn **vah**-gon
I'm retired:	Ja sam u mirovini	ya sahm oo mee-rau-**vee**-nee
to return (go back)	vratiti se	**vrah**-tee-tee se
(to give back)	vratiti	**vrah**-tee-tee
return ticket	povratna karta	pau-vrah-tnah **kahr**-tah
rice	riža (f)	**ree**-zhah
rich	bogat(a)(o)	**bau**-gaht

English	Croatian	Pronunciation
right (correct)	točan(čna)(čno)	**tautch**-an
right	desni(a)(o)	**des**-nau
at/to the right	na desno	nah **des**-nau
to ring (bell)	pozvoniti	pauz-**vau**-nee-tee
(phone)	pozvati	**pau**-zvah-tee
ring	prsten (m)	**prs**-ten
ring road	kružna autocesta	**kroozh**-nah ow-toh-**tse**-stah
road (in town)	ulica (f)	**oo**-lee-tsah
road map	autokarta	a-oo-tau-**kahr**-tah
road sign	prometni znak	pro-met-nee **znahk**
roast	pečen(a)(o)	**pe**-tche-nau
roll (bread)	pecivo (n)	**pe**-tsee-vau
room (hotel)	hotelska soba	**hau**-tel-skah **sau**-bah
(space)	prostor (m)	**prau**-staur
double room	dvokrevetna soba	**dvau**-kre-vet-nah **sau**-bah
family room	obiteljska soba	au-**bee**-tely-skah

English	Croatian	Pronunciation
single room	soba jednokrevetna soba	sau-bah, yed-nau-kre-vet-nah sau-bah
room number	broj sobe	brauy sau-be
room service	sobna usluga	saub-nah oos-loo-gah
rose	ruža (f)	roo-zhah
round	okruga(gla)(glo)	auk-roog-lau
row (theatre, etc)	red (m)	red
to run	trčati	tr-tchah-tee

S

English	Croatian	Pronunciation
sad	tužan(žna)(žno)	too-zhan
safe (for valuables)	trezor (m)	treh-zaur
safe (medicine, etc)	bezopasan (sna)(sno)	bez-au-pahs-nau
safety	sigurnost (f)	see-goor-naust
salad	salata (f)	sah-lah-tah
green salad	zelena salata	ze-le-nah

English	Croatian	Pronunciation
		sah-lah-tah
mixed salad	miješana salata	meeye-shah-nah
		sah-lah-tah
salami	salama (f)	sah-lah-mah
sale (reductions)	rasprodaja (f)	ras-prau-da-ya
salesman/woman	prodavač(-ica)	prau-dah-vatch
salt	sol (f)	saul
salty	slan(a)(o)	slah-nau
same	isti(a)(o)	ees-toh
sand	pijesak (m)	pee-ye-sahk
sandwich	sendvič (m)	send-veetch
toasted sandwich	tostiran sendvič	toh-stee-ran send-veetch
satellite dish	satelitska antena	sah-te-leet-skah ahn-te-nah
satellite TV	satelitska televizija	sah-te-leet-skah te-le-vee-zee-ya
Saturday	subota (f)	soo-bau-tah

English – Croatian

English	Croatian	Pronunciation
sauce	umak (m)	**oo**-mahk
to save (life)	spasiti život	**spah**-see-tee **zhee**-vaut
(money)	štedjeti novac	šteh-**dye**-tee
savoury (not sweet)	slano	slah-noh
to say	reći	**re**-chee
scarf (headscarf)	šal (m)	shahl
	marama (f)	**mah**-rah-mah
school	škola (f)	**shkau**-lah
Scotland	Škotska	**shkaut**-skah
Scottish	Škotski(a)(o)	**shkaut**-skee
sculpture	skulptura (f)	skool-**ptoo**-rah
sea	more (n)	**mau**-re
seafood	morski plodovi	**maur**-skee **plau**-dau-ve
to search	tragati	**trah**-gah-tee
sea sickness	morska	**maur**-skah
	bolest	**bau**-lest
seaside: at the seaside	primorje: na primorju	**pree**-maur-ye: nah **pree**-maur-yoo
season (of year)	sezona (f)	se-**zau**-nah
seasonal	sezonski(a)(o)	se-zaun-skee
season ticket	sezonska karta	se-zaun-skah kahr-tah
seat (chair)	stolica (f)	stau-lee-tsah
(theatre, plane)	sjedalo (n)	sye-dah-loh
seatbelt	pojas (m)	pau-yas
second (time)	sekunda (f)	se-**koon**-dah
second class	drugi razred	droo-gee rahz-red
to see	vidjeti	**veed**-ye-tee
to sell	prodati	prau-**dah**-tee
do you sell...?	Prodajete li...?	prau-**dah**-ye-te lee...?
to send	poslati	**paus**-lah-tee
serious (not funny)	ozbiljan(na)(no)	auz-bee-lyan
	nije smiješno	nee-ye smee-**yesh**-nau

English	Croatian	Pronunciation
to serve	uslužiti	oos-**loozh**-ee-tee
several	nekoliko	ne-kau-lee-koh
sex (gender)	spol (m)	spaul
shade	sjena (f)	**sye**-nah
to shake (bottle)	mućkati	**moo**-chkah-tee
shampoo	šampon (m)	**shahm**-paun
to share	dijeliti	dee-**ye**-lee-tee
sharp (razor, blade)	oštar	**aush**-tahr
to shave	brijati se	**bree**-yah-tee se
shaver	britvica (f)	**breet**-vee-tsah
she	ona (f)	**au**-nah
sheet (bed)	plahta (f)	**plah**-h-tah
shellfish	školjka (f)	**shko**-lykah
sheltered	zaklonjen (m/f) a/o	**zah**-kloh-nyen
to shine	blistati	**blee**-stah-tee
shirt	košulja (f)	**kau**-shoo-lyah
shoe	cipela (f)	**tsee**-pe-lah
shop	dućan (m); prodavaonica (f)	**doo**-chahn; prau-dah-**vow**-nee-tsah

English	Croatian	Pronunciation
to shop	kupovati	koo-**pau**-vah-tee
shop assistant	prodavač(ica)	prau-dah-**vah**-tch
short (person)	kratak(tka)(tko)	**kraht**-koh
	niska	**nees**-kah
	osoba (f)	**aus**-au-bah
shorts	kratke	**kraht**-ke
	hlače (n)	**hlah**-tche
shoulder	rame (n)	**rah**-me
to shout	vikati	**vee**-kah-tee
show (theatre)	predstava (f)	**pred**-stah-vah
to show	pokazati	pau-**kah**-zah-tee
shower (rain)	tuš (m)	toosh
	pljusak (m)	**plyoo**-sahk
to shrink	smanjiti (a/o)	smah-**nyee**-tee se
shut (closed)	zatvoren(a)(o)	**zaht**-vau-re-nau
sick (ill)	bolestan(sna) (sno)	**bau**-les-tahn
side	strana (f)	**strah**-nah
sightseeing	razgledanje (n)	rahz-**gle**-dah-nye

English – Croatian

tour			gospodin (m)	gaus-**pau**-deen
sign	znak (m)	znahk	sir	
(on road)	prometni znak	prau-**met**-nee **znahk**		sestra (f)	**ses**-trah
to sign	potpisati	paut-**pee**-sah-tee	sister		sye-**dee**-tee
signature	potpis (m)	paut-pees	to sit	sjediti	
silk	svila (f)	**svee**-lah	please,	Molim,	**mau**-leem,
silver	srebro (n)	**sreb**-rau	sit down	sjednite	**syed**-nee-te
similar	slično	**sleetch**-nau	size (of clothes, shoes)	veličina (f); broj (m)	ve-lee-**tchee**-nah; brauy
since (time)	otkada	**aut**-kah-dah	to ski	skijati	**skee**-ya-tee
to sing	pjevati	**pye**-vah-tee	skis	skije (f)	**skee**-ye
single	neudana (f);	ne-**oo**-dah-nah;	ski instructor	instruktor(ica)	een-strook-taur
(unmarried)	neoženjen (m)	ne-**au**-zhe-nyen		skijanja	**skee**-yah-nyah
(not double)			skin	koža (f)	**kau**-zhah
	jednokrevetan (na)	yed-**noh**-kre-vet-an	skirt	suknja (f)	**sook**-nyah
(ticket)	u jednom smjeru	oo **yed**-naum smye-roo	sky	nebo (n)	**ne**-bau
			to sleep	spavati	**spah**-vah-tee
single bed	krevet za jednu osobu	**kreh**-vetzah yeh-dnuh **au**-soh-boo	to sleep in	spavati u krišķa (f)	**spah**-vah-tee **oo** **kree**-shkah
single room	jednokrevetna soba	yed-**noh**-kre-vet-nah **sau**-bah	slice (piece of)	sličića (f)	**slee**-tchee-tsah
			slide (photo)	spor(a)(o)	**spau**-rau
			slow	usporiti	oos-**pau**-ree-tee
			to slow down	polako	pau-**lah**-koh
			slowly		

small	malen(a)(o)	mah-**leh**-nau	soft drink	rijetki sok	ree-**yet**-kee **sauk**
smell (pleasant)	miris (m)	**mee**-rees	some (a few)	neki(a)(o); par; nekoliko	**ne**-kee pahr; ne-kau-lee-koh
smell (bad)	smrditi	sm-**rhdee**-tee			
to smell of	mirisati na	mee-**ree**-sah-te nah	someone	netko	**net**-koh
			something	nešto	**ne**-shtoh
smile	osmijeh (m)	**aus**-mee-yeh	sometimes	nekad	**ne**-kahd
to smile	smjehiti se	**smye**-shee-tee se	son	sin (m)	seen
smoke	dim (m)	deem	song	pjesma (f)	**pyes**-mah
to smoke	pušiti	**poo**-shee-tee	soon	uskoro	**oos**-kau-rau
smooth	gladak(tka)(tko)	gla-dahk	as soon as possible	što prije moguće	shtoh **pree**-ye mau-**goo**-che
snack	zakuska (f)	**zah**-koos-kah	sore throat	bolno grlo (n)	**baul**-nau **gr**-lau
to sneeze	kihati	**kee**-hah-tee	sorry: *I'm sorry!*	Žao mi je!	**zhow mee** ye!
snow	snijeg (m)	**snee**-yeg			
to snow: *it's snowing*	snijeg pada	**snee**-yeg**pah**-dah	soup	juha (f)	**yoo**-hah
soap	sapun (m)	**sah**-poon	south	jug (m)	yoog
sober	mamuran(rna)(rno)	**mah**-moo-rahn	souvenir	suvenir (m)	**soo**-ve-neer
sofa	trosjed (m)	**trau**-syed	space (parking)	prostor (m); parkiralište (n)	**praus**-taur; pahr-**kee**-rah-
soft	mek(a)(o)	mek			

English – Croatian

English	Croatian	Pronunciation
sparkling	pjenušav(a)(o)	pye-**noo**-shah-v
to speak	govoriti	**gau**-vau-ree-tee
do you speak English?	Govorite li engleski?	**lee eng**-les-kee?
special	poseban(bna)	pau-seb-nau
speciality (m)	specijalitet (m)	spe-tsee-ya-lee-tet
speed	brzina (f)	br-**zee**-nah
speed limit	ograničenje brzine	**au**-grah-nee-tche-nye brz-**ee**-ne
speeding	prebrza vožnja	preh-brz-**ah** vozh-nyah
to spell	pisati	**pee**-sah-tee
how's it spelt?	Kako se to piše?	**kah**-koh se pee-she?
to spend	potrošiti	paut-trau-shee-tee
spice	začin (m)	**zah**-tcheen

English	Croatian	Pronunciation
spicy	začinjen(a)(o)	**zah**-tchee-nye-nau
to spill	proliti	**prau**-lee-tee
spinach	špinat (m)	**shpee**-naht
spirits (alcohol)	žestoka pića	**zhes**-toh-kah **pee**-chah
spoon	žlica (f)	**zhlee**-tsah
sport	šport (m)	shpaurt
sports shop	športska odjeća	**shpaur**-tskah **aud**-ye-chah
spot (stain)	mrlja (f)	**mr**-lyah
spring (place)	mjesto (n)	**mye**-stau
spring (season)	proljeće (n)	**prau**-lye-che
(metal)	opruga (f)	**aup**-roo-gah
square (in town)	trg (m)	trg
to squeeze	stisnuti	**stees**-noo-tee
stadium	stadion	**stah**-dee-on
staff	osoblje (n)	**aus**-aub-lye
stairs	stepenice (f)	**ste**-pe-nee-tse
stamp	marka (f)	**mahr**-kah
to stand	stajati	**stah**-ya-tee
star	zvijezda (f)	zvee-**yez**-dah

English	Croatian	Pronunciation
start	početak (m)	pau-**tche**-tahk
to start	početi	**pau**-tche-tee
starter (food)	predjelo (n)	**pred**-ye-lau
station	kolodvor (m)	**kau**-laud-vaur
statue	kip (m)	keep
stay	boraviti	**bau**-rah-vee-tee
enjoy your stay!	Uživajte u boravku!	**oo**-zhee-vahy-te ooh **bau**-rah-vhku!
to stay (remain)	ostati	**aus**-tah-tee
steak	odrezak (m)	**aud**-re-zahk
to steal	ukrasti	**ook**-rahs-tee
to steam	obariti	au-**bah**-ree-tee
steep: is it steep?	Je li to strmo?	ye lee **str**-mau?
step (stair)	stepenica (f)	**ste**-pe-nee-tsa
stereo	stereo (m)	**ste**-reo
sterling	funta (f)	**foon**-tah
to stick	zalijepiti	zah-**lee**-ye-

English	Croatian	Pronunciation
(with glue)		pee-tee
still (motionless)	nepomičan (m); nepomična (f)	**ne**-pau-mee-tchahn; **ne**-paum-eetch-nah
(water)	izvorski(a)(o)	**eez**-vaur-skah
(jet)	mlaz (m)	mlahz
stolen	ukradeno	ook-**rah**-de-nau
stomach	trbuh (m)	**tr**-booh
stomachache	bol u trbuhu	**baul** oo **tr**-boo-hoo
stone	kamen (m)	**kah**-men
to stop (come to a halt)	stati	**stah**-tee
(stop doing something)	prestati	**pres**-tah-tee
stop sign	stop znak	stop **znahk**
store (shop)	dućan (f)	doo-chan
storey	kat (m)	kaht
storm	oluja (f)	au-**loo**-yah
story	priča (f)	**pree**-tchah
straightaway	odmah	oh-dmah

English – Croatian

straight on	ravno	**rahv**-nau	stupid	glup(a)(o)	gloop-p
strange	čudnovat(a)(o)	**tchood**-nau-vah-toh	suddenly	iznenada	**eez**-ne-nah-dah
straw (drinking)	slamka (f)	**slahm**-kah	sugar	šećer (m)	**she**-cher
strawberries	jagode (f)	**yah**-gau-de	sugar-free	bez šećera	bez **she**-che-rah
street	ulica (f)	**oo**-lee-tsah	to suggest	predložiti	preh-dlau-jee-tee
street map	karta grada (f)	**kahr**-tah grah-**da**	suit (man's)	odijelo (n)	**aud**-ee-ye-lau
			suitcase	putna torba (f)	**kaus**-teem
				poot-nah	**poot**-nah
strength (of person)	snaga (f)	**snah**-gah	sum (of money)	iznos (f)	**taur**-bah
(of wine)	jačina (f)	**yah**-tch-**ee**-nah	summer	ljeto (n)	**eez**-nos
stress	napetost (f)	**nah**-pe-taust	sun	sunce (n)	**lye**-toh
stroke (medical)	moždani udar	**mozh**-danee **oo**-dahr	to sunbathe	sunčati se	**soon**-tse
			sunbeam	sunčani zrak (m)	**soon**-tchah-tee-se
					soon-tchah-nee **zrahk**
strong	snažan(žna)(žno)	**snahzh**-an	sunburn	opeklina od sunca	au-pek-lee-nah
strong coffee	jaka kava (f)	**yah**-kah **kah**-vah			**aud soon**-tsah
strong tea	jaki čaj (m)	**yah**-kee tchay	suncream	krema za sunce	**kre**-mah **zah**
student	student(ica) (m)	**stoo**-dent			**soon**-tse
student	studentski	**stoo**-dent-skee	Sunday	nedjelja (f)	**ned**-ye-lyah
discount	popust	**pau**-poost	sunglasses	naočale za	**now**-tcha-le-zah
stuffed	punjen(a)(o)	**poo**-nye-n			

English	Croatian	pronunciation
	je...	je...
	iznenađenje (n)	eez-**ne**-nah-**je**-nye
sunny:	sunce	**soon**-tse
it's sunny	Sunčano je	**soon**-tchah-nau **ye**
sunrise	izlazak	**eez**-lah-zahk
sunscreen	sunca (m)	**soon**-tsah
sunset	sjenilo (n)	**sye**-nee-lau
	zalazak	**zah**-lah-zahk
sunshade	sunca (m)	**soon**-tsah
sunstroke	suncobran (m)	**soon**-tsau-brahn
	sunčanica (f)	**soon**-**tchah**-nee-tsah
supermarket	samoposluga (f)	**sah**-mau-**paus**-loo-gah
supper (dinner)	večera (f)	ve-**tche**-rah
supplement	dodatak (f)	dau-**dah**-tahk
to supply	dodavati	dau-**dah**-vah-tee
sure	sigurno	**see**-goor-nau
I'm sure	siguran(rna) (rno)	**see**-goo-rahn
surname	prezime (n)	**pre**-zee-me
my surname	Moje prezime	**moy**-e **pre**-zee-

English	Croatian	pronunciation
is...	je...	
surprise	iznenađenje (n)	eez-**ne**-nah-**je**-nye
to survive	opstati	**aup**-stah-tee
to swear (bad language)	psovati	**psau**-vah-tee
to sweat	znojiti se	**znau**-yee-tee se
sweet (not savoury)	sladak(tka) (tko)	**slah**-dahk
sweetener	zasladivac (m)	zah-**slah**-djivatch
sweets	bomboni (m)	**baum**-bau-nee
to swell	oteći	o-**teh**-chee
to swim	plivati	**plee**-vah-tee
swimming pool	bazen (m)	**bah**-zen
swimsuit	kupaći	**koo**-pah-chee
	kostim (m)	**kaus**-teem
to switch off	isključiti	eesk-**lyoo**-tchee-tee
to switch on	uključiti	ook-**lyoo**-tchee-tee

English – Croatian

English – Croatian

swollen	natečeno	nah-**te**-tche-nau			nah
T			taste (clothes)	ukus (m) *or*	**oo**-koos
table	stol (m)	staul		okus (m)	oh-koos
tablet (pill)	pilula (f)	**pee**-loo-lah	to taste	kušati	**koo**-shah-tee
table tennis	stolni tenis (m)	**staul**-nee **te**-nees	tax	porez (m)	**pau**-rez
table wine	stolno vino (n)	**staul**-nau **vee**-nau	taxi	taksi (m)	**tah**-ksee
to take (carry)	nositi	**nau**-see-tee	tea	čaj (m)	tchay
(to grab, seize)	dograbiti	**daug**-rah-bee-tee	herbal tea	biljni čaj (m)	**bee**-lynee tchay
how long does	Koliko dugo	**kau**-lee-koh **doo**-	to teach	podučavati	**pau**-doo-**tchah**-vah-tee
it take?	to traje?	gau toh **trah**-ye?	teacher	učiteljica (f)	**oo**-tchee-tely
takeaway (food)	hrana za	**hrah**-nah zah	team	momčad (m);	maum-tchahd;
	ponijeti	**pon**-eeye-tee		ekipa (f)	e-kee-pah
to take off	skinuti	**skee**-noo-tee se;	teaspoon	žličica (f)	**zhlee**-tchee-tsah
	svući se	**svoo**-chee se	teeth	zubi (m)	**zoo**-bee
to take out	izvaditi	**eez**-vah-dee-tee	telephone	telefon (m)	te-**le**-faun
(of bag)			to telephone	telefonirati	te-le-fau-**nee**-rah-tee
to talk	razgovarati	**rahz**-gau-**vah**-rah-tee	telephone	telefonska	te-le-**faun**-skah
tall	visok(a)(o)	**vee**-sauk	box	kabina (f)	kah-**bee**-nah
tangerine	mandarina (f)	**mahn**-dah-**ree**-	telephone	telefonski	te-le-**faun**-skee

English	Croatian	Pronunciation
call	poziv (m)	pau-zeev
telephone card	telefonska kartica (f)	te-le-faun-skah kahr-tee-tsah
telephone number	telefonski broj (m)	te-le-faun-skee brauy
television	televizija (f)	te-le-vee-zee-yah
to tell	kazati	kah-zah-tee
temperature	temperatura (f)	tem-pe-rah-too-rah
to have a temperature	imati vrućicu	ee-mah-tee vroo-chee-tsoo
temporary	privremen(a)(o)	pree-vre-me-nau
tennis	tenis (m)	te-nees
to test (try out)	probati	prau-bah-tee
than	nego; no	ne-gau; noh
to thank	zahvaliti	zah-vah-lee-tee se
thank you	Hvala vam	hv-ah-lah vahm
thanks very much!	Hvala velika!	hv-ah-lah ve-lee-kah!
that	taj (m); ta (f);	tay; tah; toh
	to(n)	toh
theatre	kazalište (n)	kah-zah-lee-shte
theft	krađa (f)	krah-dja
their	njihov(a)(o)	nyeeh; nyee-mah
them	njih; njima	nyeeh; nyee-mah
there (over there)	tamo preko	tah-mau pre-koh
there is/	ovdje je/	auv-dye ye/
there are	ovdje su	auv-dye soo
these	ti(e)(a)	te
they	oni(e)(a)	au-nee
thick	debeo(la)(lo)	de-be-au
thief	lopov (m)	lau-pauv
thin	tanak(nka)(nko)	tah-koh
(person)	mršav(a)(o)	mr-shahv; mr-shah-vah
thing	stvar (f)	stvahr
to think	misliti	mees-lee-tee
thirsty	Žedan(dna) (dno)	he-dahn; zhed-nah
this	ovaj; ova; ovo	au-vy; au-vah; au-vau

English – Croatian

English – Croatian

English	Croatian	Pronunciation
those	ovi; ove; ova	au-vee
throat	grlo (n)	gr-lau
through	kroz	krauz
to throw away	baciti	bah-tsee-tee
thunder	grom (m)	graum
Thursday	četvrtak (m)	tche-tv-r-tahk
ticket (bus, train, etc)	putna karta (f)	poot-nah kahr-tah
(entry fee)	cijena ulaza (f)	tsee-ye-nah oo-lah-zah
a single ticket	karta u jednom smjeru	kahr-tah oo yed-naum smye-roo
a return ticket	povratna karta (f)	pauv-rah-tnah kahr-tah
ticket office	blagajna (f)	blah-gahy-nah
tidy	uredan(dna) (dno)	oo-red-nau
to tidy up	urediti	oo-re-dee-tee
tie	kravata (f)	krah-vah-tah
tight	čvrst(a)(o)	tchv-r-stau

English	Croatian	Pronunciation
till (until)	sve dok	sve dauk
time (of day)	vrijeme (n); doba dana	vree-ye-me; dau-bah dana
what time is it?	Koliko je sati?	kau-lee-koh ye sah-tee?
have you got time?	Imate li vremena?	ee-mah-te lee vre-me-nah
timetable	vozni red (m)	vauz-nee red
tip (for a waiter)	napojnica (f)	nah-pauy-nee-tsah
tired	umorna (f); umoran (m)	oo-maur-nah; oo-mau-rahn
tissues	papirnate maramice (f)	pah-peer-nateh mah-rah-mee-tse
to	do; u	dau; oo
to London	do Londona; u London	dau laun-dau-naʈ oo laun-daun
to the airport	u zračnu luku	oo zrah-tchnoo loo-koo
toast (to eat)	tost (f)	tohst
(raising glass)		oo trhast!

English	Croatian	
tobacco	duhan (m)	**doo**-hahn
tobacconist's	duhan (m)	**doo**-hahn
today	danas	**dah**-nahs
together	zajedno	zah-**yed**-nau
toilet	zahod (m)	**zah**-h-aud
tomato	rajčica (f)	**rahy**-tchee-tsah
tomorrow	sutra	**soo**-trah
tomorrow morning	sutra ujutro	**soo**-trah oo-yoo-trau
tomorrow afternoon	sutra popodne	**soo**-trah **pau**-paud-ne
tomorrow evening	sutra navečer	**soo**-trah nah-ve-tcher
tongue	jezik (m)	**ye**-zeek
tonic water	tonik (m)	**tau**-neek
tonight	večeras	ve-**tche**-rahs
too (also)	također	tah-**kau**-jer
too big	prevelik(a)(o)	**pre**-ve-leek
too small	premalen(a)(o)	**pre**-mah-len
too hot	prevruć(a)(e)	**pre**-vrooch
too noisy	prebučan	**pre**-booch-an

English	Croatian	
tooth	zub (m)	zoob
toothache	zubobolja (f)	zoo-**bau**-bau-lyah
toothbrush	četkica za zube (f)	**tchet**-kee-tsah zah **zoo**-be
toothpaste	pasta za zube (f)	**pahs**-tah zah **zoo**-be
top: the top floor	zadnji kat	zah-dnyee **kaht**
total	ukupan(pna) (pno)	**oo**-koop-an
to touch	taknuti	**tahk**-noo-tee
tough (meat)	tvrdo; žilavo meso	**tvr**-dau; **zhee**-lah-vau **me**-sau
tour	kružni izlet (m)	**kroozh**-nee **eez**-let
tourist	turist (m)	**too**-reest
tourist board	turistička zajednica	too-**rees**-teetch-kah **zah**-yed-

English – Croatian

English	Croatian	pronunciation
tourist information	turistički podaci	nee-tsah too-**rees**-teetch-kee **pah**-dah-tsee
tourist office	turistički ured (m)	too-**rees**-teetch-kee **oo**-red
tower	toranj (m)	**tau**-rahny
town	grad (m); mjesto (n)	grahd; **myes**-toh
town centre	centar grada (m)	**tsen**tar**grah**dah
town hall	vijećnica (f)	**vyech**-nee-tsah
town plan	plan grada (m)	**plahn grah**-dah
toxic	otrovan(vna)(vno) (n)	**aut**-rauv-ahn; **aut**-rauv-nah; **aut**-rauv-noh
toy	igračka (f)	**eeg**-rahtch-kah
toy shop	prodavaonica igračaka (f)	prau-dah-**vow**-nee-tsah **eeg**-rah-tchah-kah
traditional	tradicionalan (lna)(lno)	**trah**-dee-**tseo**-nahl-nau

English	Croatian	pronunciation
traffic	promet (m)	**prau**-met
traffic jam	zastoj u prometu	**zah**-stauy **oo** **prau**-me-too
traffic lights	semafor (m)	se-mah-faur
traffic warden	pozornik (m)	pau-zaur-neek vlahk
train	vlak (m)	ee-doo-che vlahk
the next train	idući vlak (m)	pr-vee **vlahk**
the first train	prvi vlak (m)	zahd-nyee **vlahk**
the last train	zadnji vlak (m)	**trahm**-vahy
tram	tramvaj (m)	**pre**-ves-tee
to translate	prevesti	**poo**-tau-vah-tee
to travel	putovati	too-**rees**-teetch-kah ah-**gen**-tsee-ya
travel agent's	Turistička agencija	
trip	izlet (m)	**eez**-let
trolley	kolica (f)	**kau**-lee-tsah
trouble	problem (m)	**praub**-lem
trousers	hlače (n)	**hlah**-tche
true	istinit(a)(o)	**ees**-tee-nee-t

English	Croatian	
to try	pokušati probati	**pau**-koo-shah-tee **prau**-bah-tee
to try on (clothes, etc)		
t-shirt	majica (f)	**mah**-yee-tsah
Tuesday	utorak (m)	**oo**-tau-rahk
to turn (handle, wheel)	pokrenuti	pau-**kre**-noo-tee
to turn around	okrenuti	au-**kre**-noo-tee
to turn off (light, etc)	isključiti	ees-**klyoo**-tchee-tee
(tap)	zavrnuti	zah-**vr**-noo-tee
to turn on (light, etc)	upaliti	oo-**pah**-lee-tee
(tap)	odvrnuti	aud-**vr**-noo-tee
turquoise (colour)	tirkizan(a)(o)	teer-keez-an
twice	dvaput	**dvah**-poot
twin beds	dva kreveta	dvah kreh-veh-ta
typical	tipičan(čna)(čno)	tee-**peetch**-nau

U

English	Croatian	
ugly	ružan(žna)(žno)	**roozh**-an
umbrella (sunshade)	kišobran (m)	**kee**-shau-brahn soon-tsau-brahn
uncle	suncobran (m) stric; ujak (m)	streets; **oo**-yahk
uncomfortable	neudoban (bna)(bno)	ne-**oo**-dob-an
under	ispod	ees-paud
underground (metro)	podzemna željeznica	paud-zem-nah **zhe**-lyez-nee-tsah
to understand	razumjeti	rah-**zoo**-mye-tee
I don't understand	Ne razumijem	ne rah-**zoo**-mee-yem
do you understand?	Da li razumijete?	dah lee rah-**zoo**-mee-ye-te?
underwear	donje rublje (n)	**dau**-nye **roob**-lye
to undress	skinuti se	skee-noo-tee se
unemployed	nezaposlen (a)(o) (f)	ne-**zah**-paus-len
to unfasten	otkopčati	ot-**kaup**-tchah-tee
United	Ujedinjeno	oo-**ye**-dee-nye-nau

English – Croatian

English	Croatian	Pronunciation
Kingdom	Kraljevstvo (n)	krah-lyev stvau
university	sveučilište (n)	sve-oo-tchee-leesh-te
unlikely	malo vjerojatno	mah-lau vye-rau-yaht-nau
to unlock	otključati	ot-klyoo-tchah-tee
to unpack	otpakirati	ot-pah-keee-rah-tee
unpleasant	neugodan (dna)(dno)	ne-oo-gaud-an
until	sve do; sve dok	sve dau; sve dauk
unusual	neobično	ne-au-beetch-nau
up: to get up	ustati	oos-tah-tee
urgent	hitan(tna)(tno)	heet-nau
us	nas; nam	nahs; nahm
to use	koristiti	kau-ree-stee-tee
useful	koristan (sna)(sno)	kau-rees-nau
usual	uobičajen (a)(o)	oo-au-bee-tcha-yehn
usually	obično	au-beetch-nau

V

English	Croatian	Pronunciation
vacancy (in hotel)	slobodna soba	slau-baud-na soh-bah
vacant	slobodan (dna)(dno)	slau-bau-dahn
valid	važeći(a)(e)	vah-zhe-che
valuable	vrijedan	vree-yed-an
value	vrijednost (f)	vree-yed-naust
VAT	PDV	pe-de-ve
vegetables	povrće (n)	pau-vr-che
vegetarian	vegetarijanac (nka)	ve-ge-tah-ree-yah-nats
ventilator	rashladivač (m)	rahs-hlah-jee-vahtch
very	vrlo	vr-lau
view	pogled (m)	paug-led
villa	vila (f)	vee-lah
village	selo (n)	se-lau
vinegar	ocat (m)	au-tsaht

virus	virus (m)	vee-roos
visa	viza (f)	vee-zah
visit	posjet (f)	paus-yet
to visit	posjetiti	paus-sye-tee-tee
visitor	posjetitelj (m)	paus-ye-tee-tely
voice	glas (m)	glahs
volcano	vulkan (m)	vool-kahn
to vomit	povratiti	pau-**vrah**-tee-tee
voucher	kupon (m)	**koo**-pon

W

to wait (for)	čekati	**tche**-kah-tee
waiter/	konobar/	kau-nau-bahr/
waitress	konobarica	kau-nau-**bah**-ree-tsah
waiting room	čekaonica (f)	tchek-**ow**-nee-tsah
to wake up (someone)	probuditi	prau-**boo**-dee-tee
(oneself)	probuditi se	prau-**boo**-dee-tee se

Wales	Vels	vels
walk	hod (m)	haud
to walk	hodati	**hau**-dah-tee
wall	zid (m)	zeed
wallet	novčanik (m)	nauv-**tcha**-neek
to want	željeti	**zhe**-lye-tee
I want...	Ja želim...	ya **zhe**-leem...
we want...	Mi želimo...	mee **zhe**-lee-mau...
warm	topao(pla) (plo)	**tau**-pow; **taup**-lah
it's warm	toplo je	**tau**-plau ye
to warm up (milk, etc)	ugrijati	oo-gree-**yah**-tee
to wash	oprati	**aup**-rah-tee
(to wash oneself)	oprati se	**aup**-rah-tee se
wasp sting	žaoka ose (f)	**zhow**-kah **au**-se
watch	ručni sat (m)	**rootch**-nee saht

English – Croatian

English – Croatian

English	Croatian	Pronunciation
to watch	gledati	gle-dah-tee
water	voda (f)	vau-dah
mineral water	mineralna voda (f)	mee-ne-rahl-nah vau-dah
sparkling water	gazirana voda (f)	gah-zee-rah-nah vau-dah
still water	negazirana voda (f)	ne-gah-zee-rah-nah vau-dah
watermelon	lubenica (f)	luh-beh-nee-tsah
way in	ulaz (m)	oo-lahz
way out	izlaz (m)	eez-lah-zahk
we	mi	mee
weak	slab(a)(o)	slahb
weak (person)	slabić (m)	slah-beech
(tea, coffee, etc)	slab čaj (m); slaba kava (f)	slahb tchay; slah-bah kah-vah
to wear	nositi	nau-see-tee
weather	vrijeme (n)	vree-ye-me
weather forecast	prognoza vremena (f)	praug-nau-zah vre-me-nah
wedding	svadba (f)	svahd-bah
Wednesday	srijeda (f)	sree-ye-dah
week	tjedan (m)	tye-dahn
last week	prošli tjedan (m)	prau-shlee tye-dahn
next week	idući tjedan (m)	ee-doo-chee tye-dahn
per week	tjedno	tye-dnnoh
this week	ovaj tjedan (m)	au-vahy tye-dahn
weekend	vikend (m)	veek-end
next weekend	idući vikend (m)	ee-doo-chee veek-end
this weekend	ovaj vikend (m)	au-vahy veek-end
weekly	tjedno	tyed-noh
to weigh	vagati	vah-gah-tee
weight	težina (f)	te-zhee-nah
welcome	dobrodošli	daub-rau-daush-lee
well	dobro	daub-rau
well-done (steak)	dobro pečen	daub-rau peh-tchen

English	Croatian	Pronunciation
Welsh	velški (m)	shee-rau-k
west	zapad (m)	shee-**ree**-nah
wet	mokar(kra)(kro)	**zhe**-nah;
what	što	**soop**-roo-gah
what is it?	Što je to?	pau-bee-**ye**-dee-tee
when	kad	
where	gdje	**vye**-tahr
which	koji (m); koja (f); koje (n)	**prau**-zaur
		eez-laug
while	dok	vye-**trau**-vee-toh ye!
in a while	uskoro	
whipped cream	šlag (m)	**vee**-nau
whisky	viski (m)	tsr-nau **vee**-nau
white	bijelo	bee-ye-lau **vee**-nau
who	tko	
wholemeal bread	čitav(a)(o) kruh (m)	**soo**-hau **vee**-nau
		slah-tkoh **vee**-nau
whose: *whose is it?*	Čije je to?	ro-**ze**; tsr-**ve**-nau **vee**-nau
why	zašto	pye-**noo**-shah-

wide	**vel**-shkee
width	**zah**-pahd
wife	**mauk**-ahr
to win	shtoh ye toh?
wind	gdye
window (shop)	**kau**-ye: **kau**-ya; **kau**-ye?
windy: *it's windy*	dauk-
wine	**oosko**-roh
red wine	shlahg
white wine	**vees**-kee
dry wine	bee-**ye**-lau tkoh?
sweet wine	**tchee**-tah-vah krooh
rosé wine	**chee**-ye ye toh?
sparkling	**zhah**-shtoh

English – Croatian

English	Croatian	Pronunciation
wine	vino (n)	vau **vee**-nau
winter	zima (f)	**zee**-mah
with	sa; s	sah; s
with ice	s ledom	s **le**-daum
with milk	s mlijekom	s **mlee**-ye-kaum
with sugar	sa šećerom	sah **she**-che-raum
without	bez	bez
without ice	bez leda	bez **le**-dah
without milk	bez mlijeka	bez **mlee**-ye-kah
without sugar	bez šećera	bez **she**-che-rah
woman	žena (f)	**zhe**-nah
wonderful	čudesan(sna) (sno)	**choo**-des-an
word	riječ (f)	ree-**yetch**
work	rad (m)	rahd
to work	raditi	**rah**-dee-tee
world	svijet (m)	svee-**yet**
worried	zabrinut(a)(o)	zah-**bree**-noo-t
worse	lošije	**lau**-shee-ye
to wrap up	zamotati	zah-**mau**-tah-tee
(parcel)		
to write	pisati	**pee**-sah-tee
please write it down	Molim, napišite to	**mau**-leem, **nah**-pee-shee-te toh
wrong	pogrešan(šna) (šno)	**paug**-re-shan
what's wrong?	Što je pogrešno?	shtoh ye **pau**-gresh-nau?

X

English	Croatian	Pronunciation
x-ray	rendgen (m)	**ren**-dgen
to x-ray	snimiti	**snee**-mee-tee
	rendgenom	**ren**-dgen-ohm

Y

English	Croatian	Pronunciation
Year	godina (f)	**gau**-dee-nah
this year	ova godina (f)	**au**-vah gau-dee-nah
next year	iduća godina (f)	**gau**-dee-nah ee-doo-cha

last year	prošla godina (f)	gau-dee-nah praush-lah
yearly	(every year)	gau-dee-nah svah-ke
yellow	žut(a)(o)	gau-dee-ne zhoo-tah
Yellow Pages	Telefonski Imenik	te-le-**faun**-skee ee-men-eek
yes	da	dah
yesterday	jučer	**yoo**-tcher
yet: not yet	ne još	**ne** yoosh
yoghurt (m)	jogurt (m)	**yau**-goort
you	ti (informal); v (formal)	tee; vee
young	mlad(a)(o)	**mlah**-d
your	tvoj(a)(e) (informal); vaš(a)(e) (formal)	tvauy; vahsh

Z

zone	zona (f)	**zo**-nah
zoo	zoološki vrt (m)	zau-**au**-loh-shkee vrt

English – Croatian

Croatian - English

Croatian	English
A	
adresa (f)	address
ako	if
aktovka (f)	briefcase
alergija (f)	allergy
ali	but
ananas (m)	pineapple
aspirin(m)	aspirin
auto (m)	car
autobus (m)	bus
automehaničar (m)	garage (for repairs)
autoprijevoz (m)	transport
B	
baba (f)	grandmother; old crone
baciti	to throw away
banka (f)	bank
bankomat (m)	cash dispenser
baterija (f)	battery (car)
benzinska crpka (f)	petrol station
besplatan(a)(o)	free of charge
bez	without
bez preticanja	no overtaking
bez ulaza	no entry
PDV	VAT
bicikl (m)	bicycle
bide (n)	bidet
bijela kava (f)	white coffee
bijelo vino (n)	white wine
bilješka (f)	note
biljka (f)	plant
biti	to be
biti na odmoru	to be on holiday
blagajna (f)	cash desk; ticket office; box office
blagdan (m)	holiday
blizu	near; close by
bluza (f)	blouse
boca (f)	bottle
boja (f)	colour
bok (m)	hello! hi!
bol (f)	pain; ache
bolesna (f)	sick
bolesnik (m)	patient
bolestan (m)	ill
bolest (f)	illness; disease
bolnica (f)	hospital
bomboni (m)	sweets
bore (f)	wrinkles
brada (f)	chin
brat (m)	brother
brijačnica (f)	hairdresser
britanski(a)(o)	British
brod (m)	boat; ship
broj (m)	size (of shoe, clothes)
brz(a)(o)	quick
brzina (f)	speed
brzo	quickly

Croatian	English
bučan(čna)(čno)	noisy
budilica (f)	alarm clock
budite tihi!	Keep quiet!
budućnost (f)	future
buka (f)	noise

C

Croatian	English
centar grada (m)	city centre
cesta (f)	motorway/road
cijena (f)	price
cipele (f)	shoes
cjenovnik (m)	price list
crkva (f)	church
crn(a)(o)	black
crven(a)(o)	red
crveno vino	red wine
cura (f)	girlfriend; unmarried woman
cvijeće (n)	flowers

Croatian	English
čaj (m)	tea
čamac	boat or a dinghy
čaša	glass (for drinking)
čarape (f)	socks
ček (m)	cheque
čekati	to wait (for)
čekovna kartica (f)	cheque card
čelo (n)	forehead
često	often; frequent
četiri	four
četvrt (m)	quarter
čije je to?	Whose is it?
čistionica (f)	dry-cleaners
čist(a)(o)	clean
čitati	to read
čitav(a)(o)	whole
čokolada (f)	chocolate
čovjek (m)	man

Croatian	English
čudesan(sna)(sno)	wonderful
čudan(dna)(dno)	strange
čuti	to hear
čuvar (m)	guard
čuvati	to keep
ćelav	bald
ćevapčić (m)	small grilled meatball
ćud (m)	temperament
ćup (m)	clay jug

D

Croatian	English
da	yes
dakle	thus (in this way)
daleko	far; far away
da li	whether
da li razumijete?	Do you understand?
daljina (f)	distance

Croatian - English

Croatian – English

Croatian	English
daljinski upravljač (m)	remote control
dan (m)	day
danas	today
dar (m)	token
dati	to give
datum (m)	date; appointment
datum prodaje (m)	sell-by date
datum rodendana (m)	date of birth
davno	ago
desno	right
dežurna ljekarna (f)	duty chemists
dijabetes (m)	diabetes
dijeta (f)	diet
dijete (n)	child
dim (m)	smoke
disketa (f)	floppy disk
divno(van) (vno)	lovely; nice; pretty
djeca	children
djevojčica (f)	school girl
djevojka (f)	girl
dnevni(a)(o)	daily
dnevni boravak (m)	living room
dob (f)	age
dobar(bra)(bro)	good
dobar dan	good afternoon
dobar tek!	enjoy your meal!
dobra večer	good evening
dobro jutro	good morning
dobrodošli	welcome
doći	to come; to arrive
dodatak (m)	supplement
dogoditi se	to happen
dolazak (m)	arrivals
dom (m)	home
domaći let (m)	domestic flight
dom zdravlja	health centre
donje rublje (n)	underwear
doplatiti	to pay a supplement
dopustiti	to allow
dosta	enough
dostupan (pna)(pno)	available
dovidenja	goodbye
dozvola (f)	permit
drago mi je!	Pleased to meet you!
draguljarnica (f)	jeweller's
dragulji (m)	precious stones; jewellery
drugi	second
društvo (n)	company

državni praznik (m)	public holiday
dodati	to attach; to add
dubina (f)	depth
dubok(a)(o)	deep
dućan (m)	shop
dug (m)	debt
duhan (m)	tobacconist's
dužina (f)	length
duž ulice	along the street
dvoje (n)	couple (two people)
dvokrevetna soba (f)	double room
dvostruk(a)(o)	double

DŽ

džemper (m)	sweater
džep (m)	pocket
đak (m)	pupil (school)
đerdan (m)	necklace

E

Engleska (f)	England
Engleskinja (f)	English (woman)
Englez (m)	English (man)

F

fen (m)	hairdryer
fotograf (m)	photo shop
fotografska kamera (f)	foto camera
fotokopija (f)	photocopy
frizer (m)	hairdresser
funta (f)	sterling; pound

G

garaža (f)	garage
gdje	where
glad (m)	hunger
gladan(dna) (dno)	hungry
glasan(sna) (sno)	loud
glava (f)	head
glavni(a)(o)	main
glavni grad (m)	capital (city)
glavobolja (f)	headache
glazba (f)	music
gledalište (n)	audience; auditorium
gledati	to watch; to look at
glup(a)(o)	stupid
gljive (f)	mushrooms
godina (f)	year
gorivo (n)	fuel
gorak(rka)(rko)	bitter (taste)
gost (m)	guest
gotovina (f)	cash (money)
govoriti	to speak
grad (m)	town; city
građanin (m)	citizen

Croatian – English

Croatian	English
gradanka (f)	citizen
graditi	to build
granica (f)	boundary; border
grejpfrut (m)	grapefruit
grlo (n)	throat
groznica (f)	fever
grubo	harsh; tough
grupa (f)	group
gurati	to push

H

Croatian	English
haljina (f)	dress
hitna pomoć	accident and emergency
hlače (n)	trousers
hladno	cold
hladnjak (m)	fridge
hodati	to walk
hotel (m)	hotel
hrkati	to snore
hvala vam / hvala lijepa / puno	thank you / thanks very much
hitno	urgent

I

Croatian	English
i	and
ići	to go
ići u kupovinu	to go shopping
idemo!	Let's go!
idući(a)(e)	next
igra (f)	play; game
igrati	to play (sport)
ijedan	any
ili	or
imate li...?	do you have...?
imate li vremena?	do you have the time?
imati	to have
imati temperaturu	to have a temperature
ime (n)	name (first)
informacije (f)	information; enquiry desk
inozemstvo (n)	abroad
isključen(a)(o)	turned off
isključiti	to turn off
iskren(a)(o)	honest
iskrenost (f)	honesty
iskusan(sna)(sno)	experienced
iskustvo (n)	experience
ispit (m)	exam
ispod	under; beneath; below
ispred	in front of
ispuniti	to fill in (form)
istina (f)	truth
istinit(a)(o)	true
isto	same
istok (m)	east
išta	anything

Croatian	English				
iz	from	izvjestiti	to inform	ja sam gladan (dna)	I'm hungry
iza	behind	izvorska voda (f)	still water	ja sam žedan (dna)	I'm thirsty
izabrati	to choose	izvoziti	to export	jastučnica (f)	pillowcase
izaći	to come out	izvrstan	excellent	jastuk (m)	pillow
izbjeći	to escape			je	is (to be)
izbor (m)	choice	**J**		jedan	one
izgovarati	to pronounce	ja	I	jednak(a)(o)	equal
izgubljen(a)(o)	lost	jahati	to ride (horse)	jednokrevetna soba (f)	single room
izlaz (m)	exit; gate	ja imam...	I have...	jednosmjerna ulica (f)	one-way street
izlet (m)	excursion	ja imam ... godina	I'm ... years old	jeftin(a)(o)	cheap
izložba (f)	exhibition	ja mogu...	I can...	jelovnik (m)	menu
izložiti	to show	jakna (f)	jacket	jesti	to eat
između	among(st)	ja ne marim	I don't care	jezik (m)	language; tongue
iznad	above	ja ne mogu...	I cannot...	još	yet
iznajmiti	to let	ja ne pamtim...	I cannot remember...	još nešto	anything else
iznimka (f)	exception	ja ne pušim	I don't smoke	jučer	yesterday
izniman(mna)(mno)	exceptional	ja ne razumijem	I don't understand	jug (m)	south
izravan(vna)(vno)	direct				
izvan	outside				

Croatian – English

Croatian	English
juha (f)	soup
jutro (m)	morning
jutros	this morning
K	
kaciga (f)	helmet
kad?	when?
kako?	how?
kako se izgovara?	how is it pronounced?
kako se to piše?	how is it spelt?
kako se zovete?	what's your name?
kako ste?	how are you?
kako ide?	how's it going?
kao	as like
karta (f)	ticket; map
kasniji(a)(e)	later
kasno	late
kašljati	to cough

Croatian	English
kauč (m)	sofa bed
kava (f)	coffee
kavana (f)	coffeehouse; bar
kazalište (n)	theatre
kazati	to tell
kazna (f)	fine (to be paid)
kćer (f)	daughter
kesten (m)	chestnut
kilo/kilogram	kilo
kiša (f)	rain
kišiti	to rain
kišobran (m)	umbrella
klima tizacija (f)	air-conditioning
ključ (m)	key
knjiga (f)	book
knjižica (f)	booklet
karnet (f)	book of tickets (tram, bus)
kockati se	to gamble
kočnica (f)	brake

Croatian	English
kod	at
koji/koja/koje?	which one?
kolač (m)	cake
kolica (f)	trolley
koliko često?	how often?
koliko je sati?	what time is it?
koliko mnogo?	how many?
kompjutorska igra (f)	computer game
komarac (m)	mosquito
konac (m)	end
kondom (m)	preservative
konj (m)	horse
konoba (f)	wine cellar
konobar (m)	waiter
konobarica (f)	waitress
konopac (m)	rope
kontraceptivan (vna)(vno)	contraceptive
kontrola krvi (f)	blood test
koristan	useful

Croatian	English
koristiti	to use
kosa (f)	hair
koštati	to cost
kotač (m)	wheel
koža (f)	skin; leather
krada (f)	theft
kratak(tka) (tko)	short
kreditna kartica (f)	credit card
krimić (m)	thriller (book or film)
krov (m)	roof
kroz	through
kroz vlak	through train
kruh (m)	bread; loaf
kula (f)	tower
krumpir (m)	potato
kruška (f)	pear
kuća (f)	house
kuhan(a)(o)	cooked
kuhati	to boil; to cook
kupaći kostim (m)	swimsuit
kupka (f)	bath tub
kupiti	to buy
kupovina (f)	shopping
kušati	to taste
kvar (m)	breakdown van

L

Croatian	English
laka noć (f)	good night
lakat (m)	elbow
lako	easy
led (m)	ice
letjeti	to fly
lice (n)	face
liječnik (m)	doctor
lijek (m)	medication
lijepo	beautiful
let (m)	flight
lijevo	left
limenka (f)	tin; box
limun (m)	lemon
limunada (f)	lemonade
listopad (m)	October
litra (f)	litre
lomljiv(a)(o)	breakable
lopov (m)	thief
lopta (f)	ball
loše	badly (not well)
loše vijesti (f)	bad news
loše vrijeme (n)	bad weather
lošiji(a)(e)	worse
lud(a)(o)	mad
luk (m)	onion

LJ

Croatian	English
ljekarna (f)	chemist's; pharmacy
ljestve (f)	ladder
ljubav (f)	love
ljubičast(a)(o)	violet

Croatian – English

Croatian – English

Croatian	English
ljubiti se	to kiss
ljubomoran	jealous
ljubak(upka)(upko)o	charming
ljut	angry
ljutnja (f)	anger

M

Croatian	English
mačka (f)	cat
madrac (m)	mattress
majica (f)	vest; t-shirt
majka (f)	mother
maloljetan (tna)(tno)	underage
mama (f)	mum
malo	little
malo više	a little more
manje	less
marelica (f)	apricot
maslac (m)	butter
masline (f)	olives

Croatian	English
material (m)	material
mediteran (m)	Mediterranean
medu	between
medunarodni (dna)(dno)	international
mek(a)(o)	smooth
meso (n)	meat
metar (m)	meter
mi idemo u...	we're going to...
mi	we
mi imamo...	we have...
mi nemamo...	we don't have...
mi možemo	we can
mi ne možemo	we cannot
mineralna voda (f)	mineral water
minimalan (lna)(lno)	minimal
misliti	to think
mjesec (m)	moon; month
mjesečni(a)(o)	monthly

Croatian	English
mjesni(a)(o)	local
mjesto (n)	town; place
mješovita roba (f)	groceries
mlad(a)(o)	young
mladić	young man
mlijeko (n)	milk
mnogo	many
mobitel (m)	mobile phone
moći	to be able (to)
modar(dra)(dro)	blue
moguće	possible
moj (m)	my; mine
moja (f)	my; mine
moje (n)	my; mine
moje prezime je...	my surname is...
molim	please
moliti krunicu	to pray with prayer beads

Croatian	English	Croatian	English	Croatian	English
momak (m)	boyfriend	najbolje prije	best before	naručiti	to order (in restaurant)
more (n)	the sea	najbolji(a)(o)	best	naslonjač (m)	armchair
most (m)	bridge	najstariji(a)(o)	oldest	nastaviti	to continue
motor (m)	engine	najveći(a)(o)	largest; greatest	nasuprot	opposite; facing
možda	perhaps; maybe	na koji način?	how? (in what way)	naš (m)	our; ours
mrkve (f)	carrots	nakon	afterwards	naša (f)	our; ours
mršav(a)(o)	thin (person)	naksutra	the day after tomorrow	naše (n)	our; ours
mrtav(tva) (tvo)	dead	nalik	like; as	natečen(a)(o)	swollen
munja (f)	thunderstorm	namještaj (m)	furniture	navika (f)	habit; manner
muškarac (m)	male	namješten (a)(o)	furnished	na vrijeme	on time
muzej (m)	museum	na odmoru	on holiday	ne	no; not
muž (m)	husband	napadati	to attack	nečist(a)(o)	unclean
		napojnica (f)	tip (to waiter)	nedavno	recently
N		na primjer	for example	ne dirati!	do not touch!
nacija (f)	nation	napustiti	to give up	nekad	then; sometimes
načinjeno od...	made of...	naranča (f)	orange	neki ljudi	some people
naći	to find	narančada	orange juice	nekoliko	several; few
nada (f)	hope			nema na čemu!	don't mention it!
nadati se	to hope			nema ulaza!	no entry!
nagovoriti	to persuade				

Croatian – English

Croatian – English

Croatian	English
nemoguće	impossible
neodgovarajuć(a)(e)	inconvenient
nepotreban (bna)(bno)	unnecessary
ne radi!	out of order!
nestati	to disappear
nešto	something
netko	someone
neugodan (dna)(dno)	uncomfortable
nije uračunat (a)(o)	excluding
nevažeći(a)(e)	invalid; expired; out-of-date
nezapaljiv(a)(o)	non-flammable
nijedan(dna) (dno)	no-one
nikad	never
nisko	low
ništa	nothing

Croatian	English
ništica (f)	zero
niti ... ni ...	neither ... nor ...
nitko	none
niz stepenice	downstairs
nizak standard	low standard
noć (f)	night
noćas	tonight
noću	at night
noga (f)	leg
nositi	to carry; to wear
nov(a)(o)	new
nova godina (f)	New Year
novac (m)	money
novčanik (m)	wallet
novčići	small coins
novina	newspaper

O

Croatian	English
objasniti	to explain
obala (f)	coast; shore
obariti	to steam (hot vapour)
obećanje (n)	promise
obećati	to promise
obično	regularly; usually
obitelj (f)	family
obiteljska soba (f)	family room
oblačno	cloudy
oblast	district; region
obnoviti	to renew
obrok (m)	meal
obrt (m)	craft; manufacture
obuća (f)	shoeshop
obućar (m)	shoemaker
obući se	to put on (clothes)
obuti se	to put on (shoes)
obvezan(zna) (zno)	compulsory

Croatian	English
ocat (m)	vinegar
očekivati	to expect
oči	eyes
odgoda (f)	postponement
odgoditi	to postpone
odgovor (m)	answer
odgovoriti	to reply; to answer
odijelo (n)	man's suit
odjeća (f)	clothes
odjednom	at once
odjel (m)	ward
odlazak (m)	departure
odlaziti	to leave
odmah	immediately
odmaralište (n)	resort
odmarati se	to rest
odrezak (m)	steak
odrezati	to cut
odsjek (m)	department
odustati	to cancel

Croatian	English
okolica (f)	surroundings
okolo	around
okončan(a)(o)	finished
okruglo	round
okupati se	to bathe (oneself)
olabavljen(a)(o)	loose (not fastened)
olovka (f)	pencil
ometati	to disturb
onesvijestiti se	to faint (oneself)
opasan(sna)(sno)	dangerous
opasnost (f)	danger
opet	again
opisati	to describe
opomena (f)	reminder
oporaviti se	to recover (from illness)
oprema (f)	equipment
oprez (m)	caution
oprostite!	excuse me!

Croatian	English
oprostiti	to forgive
organsko	organic (not food)
osiguran	to be insured
osiguranje (n)	insurance
osjećati	to feel
osoba (f)	person
osobna iskaznica (f)	identity card
osobne stvari (f)	personal belongings
osobno	private
ostali	the others
ostati	to stay; to remain
ostvariti	to realize
oštetiti	to damage
otac (m)	father
otpatci (m)	rubbish
otrovan(vna)(vno)	poisonous
otvarač (m)	bottle opener;

Croatian – English

otvarati	tin-opener	
otvoren(a)(o)	open	
otvoriti	to open	
ova (f)	this	
ovaj (m)	this	
ovaj put	this time	
ovdje	here	
ovdje je...	there is...	
ovo (n)	this	
ozbiljan(ljna)(ljno)	serious	
oženjen	married (man)	
ozljeda (f)	injury	
ožujak (m)	March	

P

padavica (f)	epilepsy	
papar (m)	pepper (spice)	
paprika (f)	pepper (vegetable)	
papreno	peppery	
papuče (f)	slippers	
par (m)	pair	
park (m)	park	
parkiralište (n)	car park	
parkirati	to park	
pas (m)	dog	
pasti	to fall	
pazi je...	take care...	
pažljivo	carefully	
pecivo (n)	bread roll	
pekarnica (f)	baker's	
pelene (f)	nappies	
petak (m)	Friday	
piće (n)	drink	
pijan	drunk	
pijesak (m)	sand	
pile (n)	chicken	
piletina (f)	chicken (meat)	
pilula (f)	tablet (pill)	
pisati	to write	

pitanje (n)	question	
pitati	to ask (a question)	
pitati za	to ask for	
piti	to drink	
pitka voda (f)	drinking water	
pivo (n)	beer	
pjenušac (m)	champagne	
pjesma (f)	song	
pješačiti	to go on foot	
pješice	on foot	
pjevati	to sing	
plaćeno	paid	
plakati	to cry	
planina (f)	mountain	
platiti novcem	to pay cash	
plato (n)	platform	
plav	blue	
plavuša (f)	blonde (woman)	
plaža (f)	beach	
ples (m)	dance	
plesati	to dance	

Croatian	English
plin (m)	gas
plinski štednjak (m)	gas cooker
plivati	to swim
pljusak (m)	shower (rain)
pobijediti	to win
poboljšati	to improve
početi	to begin
počimati	to start
podijeliti	to share
poducavati	to teach
pogreška (f)	error; mistake
pojas (m)	seatbelt
pojedinačna cijena	single fare
poklon (m)	gift
pokraj	besides
pokućstvo (n)	household articles
pola	half
pola sata	half an hour
polako	slowly
poletjeti	to take-off
policajac (m)	policeman
policija (f)	police
policijska postaja (f)	police station
pomagalo (n)	aid
pomoći	to help
ponedjeljak (m)	Monday
poništiti kartu	to validate a ticket
popodne	afternoon
popravka cipela	shoe repair
popust (m)	discount
poruka (f)	message
posao (n)	business
posjet (f)	visit
posjetiti	to visit
poslati	to send (a letter)
poslije	after
posluga (f)	service
poslužiti	to serve
posljednji	latest
postelja (f)	bed
posuditi	to lend
pošiljka (f)	packet
pošta (f)	post office
poštanski sandučić (m)	postbox
potpis (m)	signature
potpisati se	to sign
potreba (f)	need
potrošiti	to spend (money)
potvrditi	to confirm
povećati	to increase
povraćati	to vomit
povratak (m)	return
povratna karta (f)	return ticket
povrće (n)	vegetables
povući	to pull

Croatian – English

Croatian – English

Croatian	English
pozdrav (m)	greeting
poziv (m)	call (telephone)
pozvati	to invite
požar!	fire! (fire alarm)
prabaka (f)	grandmother
pradjed (m)	grandfather
praonica auta	washing cars
praonica rublja (f)	laundry (place)
prašak za rublje	detergent
prati	to wash
pravci (m)	directions
praznici (m)	public holidays; half term
prazno	empty
predstava (f)	performance (in theatre)
premoren	exhausted
preporučiti	to recommend
prepoznati	to identify
presvući se	to change one's clothes
preticati	to overtake (in car)
previše	too much
prevoditelj (m)	interpreter
prevoditi	to translate/interpret
prezime (n)	surname; family name
pridodati	to attach
prigovor (m)	complaint
prijatelj (m)	friend
prijaviti	to declare
prije	ago
prijeći ulicu	to cross the street
prikolica (f)	caravan
primiti	to receive
primjer (m)	example
primorje (n)	seaside
pripomoć (f)	assistance
pripraviti	to prepare
probati	to try out
probuditi se	to wake up
prodaja (f)	sale
prodano	sold out
prodati	to sell
prodavaonica (f)	shop
prolaznik (m)	passer-by
proliti	to spill over
proljeće (n)	spring (season)
promet (m)	traffic jam
promijeniti bateriju	to change a battery
propust (m)	fault
propušten	missed (train, plane)
prošli (a)(o)	last
protiv	against
provjeriti	to check

Croatian – English

Croatian	English
prozor (m)	window
prvi	first
pržiti	to fry
psovka (f)	swear word
pun(a)(o)	full
puna sezona	high season
pušiti	to smoke
cigarete	cigarettes
putnička agencija (f)	travel agent
putnik (m)	traveller
putovanje (n)	journey
putovati	to travel
putovnica (f)	passport

R

Croatian	English
račun (m)	account; bill; receipt
računar (m)	calculator
raditi	to work
radni stol (m)	desk
rajčica (f)	tomato
ranije	earlier
rano	early
raskrsnica (f)	crossroads
rasti	to grow
rata (f)	rate
ravnatelj (m)	manager; director
ravnateljstvo (n)	management; direction
ravno	straight on
razgledanje grada (n)	sightseeing tour
razgledati	sightseeing
razglednica (f)	postcard
razgovarati	to talk
različit(a)(o)	different
razred (m)	class
razumjeti	to understand
razviti	to develop (photos)
recepcija (f)	reception
recept (m)	prescription
red (m)	row; queue
restoran (m)	restaurant
rezervacija (f)	reservation
rezerviran(a)(o)	reserved
rezervirati	to reserve
riječ (f)	word
rizik (m)	risk
roditelji (m)	parents
roden	born
rodendan (m)	birthday
rodenje (n)	birth
roniti	to dive
roštilj (m)	grill
rubac (m)	scarf
rupčić (m)	handkerchief
ručak (m)	lunch
ručna prtljaga (f)	hand luggage
ručnik (m)	towel
ručni sat (m)	watch

Croatian – English

Croatian	English
rujan (m)	September
ruka (f)	hand; arm
ruž (m)	lipstick
ruža (f)	rose
ružan(žna) (žno)	ugly
S	
s kupaonicom	with bathroom
sad	now
salama (f)	salami
salata (f)	salad
samo	only
samoposluga (f)	supermarket
sastanak (m)	meeting
savjet (m)	advice
savjetovati	to advise
selo (n)	village
semafor (m)	traffic lights
sendvič (m)	sandwich
sestra (f)	sister
sezona (f)	season
sezonska karta (f)	season ticket
siguran(rna) (rno)	safe
sići	to get off (bus)
silaziti	to go down
sin (m)	son
sir (m)	cheese
siv(a)(o)	grey
sjedalo (n)	seat
sjednite molim	do take a seat
sjena (f)	shadow
sjever (m)	north
skijati	to ski
skok (m)	jump
skup(a)(o)	expensive
sladoled (m)	ice-cream cone
slamka (f)	straw (for drinking)
slan(a)(o)	salty
slastičarnica (f)	ice-cream shop
slijediti	to follow
slobodan ulaz (m)	free admission; free entry
slobodno	vacancy (in hotel)
slomiti	to break
slomljen(a)(o)	broken
složiti se sa	to agree with
slučajnost (f)	coincidence
slušalice (f)	headphones
slušati	listen (to)
smeće (n)	rubbish
smeđ(a)(e)	brown
smijati se	to laugh
smijeh (m)	laughter
smještaj (m)	accommodation
smrznut(a)(o)	frozen
snaga (f)	strength
snijeg (m)	snow
soba (f)	room

Croatian		English
sobarica (f)		(chamber) maid
sok (m)		juice
sol (f)		salt
spasiti		to save (life)
spavač (m)		sleeper (man)
spavaćica (f)		sleeper (woman)
spavaćica (f)		pyjamas
spavaonica (f)		bedroom
spavati		to sleep
srebro (n)		silver
srednji(a)(o)		medium; middle
sresti		to meet
sretan(tna)(tno)		happy
sretna nova godina!		Happy New Year!
srijeda (f)		Wednesday
srpanj (m)		July
stambena zgrada (f)		block of flats
stan (m)		flat; apartment
stanka (f)		interval
stanovnik (m)		inhabitant
stari(a)(o)		old
stari grad		old town
stati		to halt; to stop
stepenice (f)		stairs
sto		hundred
stoj!		stop!
stolica (f)		chair
stopala (n)		feet
stranac (m)		foreigner
stranica (f)		page
stric (m)		uncle
strina (f)		aunt
stroj za rublje (m)		washing machine
stručnjak (m)		expert
struja (f)		current (electric, water)
struk (m)		waist
studeni (m)		November
stvar (f)		thing (also a cause)
stvari za prijaviti		goods to declare
stvarno		really; actually
subota (f)		Saturday
sudnica (f)		law court
suknja (f)		skirt
sunce (n)		sun
suša (f)		draught
sušiti		to dry
sutra		tomorrow
sutra navečer		tomorrow evening
sutra popodne		tomorrow afternoon
sutra ujutro		tomorrow morning
suvremen(a)(o)		modern
svadba (f)		wedding
svaki		every

Croatian – English

Croatian – English

Croatian	English
svako dobro!	best wishes!
sve dok	until
sve u redu!	all right!
svi	all; everybody
svibanj (m)	May
svjetlo (n)	light

Š

Croatian	English
šalica (f)	mug; tea cup
šećer (m)	sugar
šešir (m)	hat
širok(a)(o)	broad
škare (f)	scissors
Škotska (f)	Scotland
škotski(a)(o)	Scottish
štednjak (m)	cooker
štedjeti	to save (money)
što?	what?
Što je to?	what is it?
što se dogodilo?	what happened?
što to znači?	what does it mean?

T

Croatian	English
ta (f)	that one
tablete za smirenje	sedative pills
tad	then
taj (m)	that one
taj put	that way
tako mnogo	so many
taknuti	to touch
tako puno	so much
tamo	there
tamo nije!	there isn't!
tamo preko	over there
tata (m)	dad
tebi	to you (informal)
tečaj (m)	course
tekućina (f)	liquid
telefonski imenik (m)	phone directory
telefonska lovornica (f)	phonebox
telefonska kartica (f)	phonecard
temperatura (f)	temperature
televizija (f)	TV programme
teretnjak (m)	lorry
termometar (m)	thermometer
termos boca (f)	thermos flask
težak(ška)(ško)	difficult; heavy
težina (f)	weight
ti	you (informal, familiar)
tih(a)(o)	calm
tiho	quietly
tiho mjesto	quiet place
tijekom	during
tisuća (f)	thousand
tišina (f)	silence

Croatian	English	Croatian	English	Croatian	English
tjedan (m)	week	trgovina (f)	shop	tvoje (n)	your; yours (informal and singular)
tjedno	weekly	trgovački centar (m)	shopping centre	tvornica (f)	factory
to	it; this	trka (f)	race	**U**	
toaletni papir (m)	toilet paper	tko?	who?	u	in; to
točeno pivo (n)	draught beer	turisti (m)	tourists	ubrus (m)	napkin
točan(čna)(čno)	right (correct)	turistička agencija (f)	tour operator	učitelj (m)	teacher
to ne radi!	it doesn't work!	turistički vodič (m)	tour guide or a tourist guide	učiti	to learn
to nije moja greška	It's not my fault	tuš (m)	shower (bathroom)	ući u	to go in; to enter; to get in (vehicle)
to nije važno!	it doesn't matter!	tužan(žna)(žno)	sad	udana	married (woman)
topla voda (f)	warm water	tvoj (m)	your; yours (informal and singular)	udati se	to get married (woman)
toplomjer (m)	thermometer	tvoja (f)	your; yours (informal and singular)	udes (m)	accident
torba (f)	bag			uđite!	come in!
tradicionalan (na)(no)	traditional			ugodan(dna)(dno)	pleasant
trajati	to last			ugrijati	to heat up
trčati	to run				
trebati	to need				
treći	third				
trg (m)	square (in town)				

Croatian – English

Croatian – English

uho *(n)*	ear	
Ujedinjeno Kraljevstvo *(n)*	United Kingdom	
ujutro	in the morning	
uključiti	to turn on (radio, TV)	
ukupan(pna) (pno)	total amount	
ukus *(m)*	taste	
ukusan(sna) (sno)	tasty	
ulaz *(m)*	entrance; entry	
ulaznica *(f)*	ticket (theatre, cinema)	
ulica *(f)*	street; road (in town)	
uliti	to pour	
ulje *(n)*	oil	
umetnuti	to insert	
umjesto	instead of	

umoran(rna) (rno)	tired	
unazad	backwards	
unovčiti	to cash (a cheque)	
unuk *(m)*	grandson	
unuka *(f)*	granddaughter	
unutra	indoors; inside	
upaliti	to switch on (light)	
upis *(m)*	enrolment; inscription	
upisati se	to join (club)	
upomoć!	help!	
uporaba *(f)*	best before!	
prije…		
upoznati se sa	to know (to be acquainted with)	
upozoriti	to warn	
upravljati volanom	to steer (car)	

uračunat(a)(o)	included	
urar *(m)*	watchmaker	
ured *(m)*	office	
uredan	tidy	
u sezoni *(f)*	in the season	
uskoro	soon	
uskrs *(m)*	Easter	
usluga *(f)*	service included	
uračunata *(f)*		
uspjeh *(m)*	success	
usta *(f)*	mouth	
ustati	to stand up; to get up	
utorak *(m)*	Tuesday	
uvijek	always	
uživati	to enjoy	

V

vadičep *(m)*	corkscrew	
vagati	to weigh	
vagon *(m)*	carriage (train)	

Croatian – English

Croatian	English
valuta (f)	currency
vama	to you (formal)
vani	outside
vanjski(a)(o)	external
vas	to you (unfamiliar)
vaš (m)	your; yours (unfamiliar)
vaša (f)	your; yours (plural and formal)
vaše (n)	your; yours (plural and formal)
vatrogasna kola (n)	fire engine
večera (f)	evening meal
večeras	tonight
veći(a)(e)	bigger; larger
većina (f)	most
vegetarijanci	vegetarians
velik(a)(o)	big; large
veljača (f)	February
ventilator (m)	fan
vi	you (formal; unfamiliar)
video snimač (m)	video recorder
vidjeti	to see
vikati	to shout
vikend (m)	weekend
vilica (f)	fork
vino (n)	wine
visina (f)	high
visok	tall
više no	more than
više volim…	I prefer…
vijećnica (f)	town hall
vjerovati	to believe
vlak (m)	train
vlasnik (m)	owner
voćna salata (f)	fruit salad
voda (f)	water
vodič (m)	guide
vozač (m)	driver
vozačka dozvola (f)	driving licence
vozilo (n)	vehicle
vrata (f)	door
vrećica čaja	tea bag
vrijedi 100 eura	worth 100 euros
vrijedno razgledanja	worth seeing
vrijednost (f)	value; worth
vrijeme (n)	time; weather
vrhnje (n)	cream
vrlo mnogo	a lot; very many
vrsta (f)	kind; type
vrt (m)	garden
vuna (f)	wool

Croatian – English

Croatian	English
Z	
za	for
zabava (f)	party
zabavno	funny (amusing)
zabavljati se	to enjoy oneself
zaboraviti	to forget
zabranjen(a)(o)	forbidden
zabranjeno parkirati!	no parking!
zabranjeno pušenje!	no smoking!
zabrinut(a)(o)	worried
zadugo	for a long time
zahod (m)	lavatory
zajam (m)	credit
zajedno	together
zakasniti na...	to miss (train, coach)
zakočiti	to brake
zašto?	why?
zato	because
zlato (n)	gold
zamijeniti novac	to change money
zamotati	to wrap up (parcel)
zamrzivač (m)	freezer
zanimanje (n)	occupation; profession
zaobilaznica (f)	ring road; diversion; detour
zapad (m)	west
zaraditi	to earn
zaručen(a)	engaged
zato...	because of...
zatvoreno	closed (shop)
zatvoreno za blagdane	closed for holidays
zavrnuti vodu	to turn off (tap)
zdravlje (n)	health
zelen(a)(o)	green (colour)
zemlja (f)	soil; country
zima (f)	winter
značenje (n)	meaning
značiti	to mean
znati	to know
zovem se...	I am called; my name is...
zračenje (n)	radiation
zračna kompanija (f)	airline
zračna luka (f)	airport
zrakoplov (m)	aircraft
zrakoplov kasni!	the plane is late!
zubna četkica	toothbrush
zubna pasta (f)	toothpaste
zvati	to call (phone)
zvonce (n)	doorbell
zvoniti	to ring a bell
zvono (n)	church bell

Ž

žao mi je!	I'm sorry!
žedan(dna) (dno)	thirsty
žeđ (f)	thirst
želja (f)	wish
željeti	to want
žena (f)	woman
živjeli!	Cheers!
živjeti	to live
život (m)	life
žlica (f)	spoon
žuriti	to hurry
žut(a)(o)	yellow (colour)
žvakati	to chew

Further titles in Collins' phrasebook range
Collins Gem Phrasebook

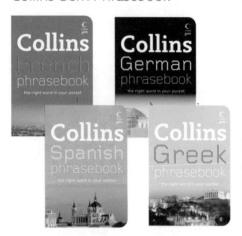

Also available as **Phrasebook CD Pack**
Other titles in the series

Arabic	Greek	Polish
Cantonese	Italian	Portuguese
Croatian	Japanese	Russian
Czech	Korean	Spanish
Dutch	Latin American	Thai
French	Spanish	Turkish
German	Mandarin	Vietnamese

Collins Phrasebook & Dictionary

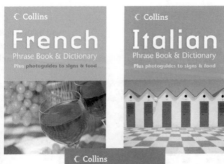

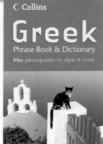

Also available as **Phrasebook CD Pack**
Other titles in the series
German Japanese Portuguese Spanish

Collins Easy: Photo Phrasebook

Also available as
Phrasebook
CD Pack

**Other titles
in the series**
Easy French
Easy Greek
Easy Italian

To order any of these titles, please telephone
0870 787 1732. For further information about all
Collins books, visit our website: www.collins.co.uk